BARBIE FAILS

Real Life Blonde Moments

Thanks to my girlfriend 'Barbie' who provided such great content and stories that I was able to create first a blog and then a book.

Acknowledgements

What started as a simple idea on day on a commuter train morphed into a blog that attracted more attention than I expected which in turn has evolved into this book in your hands.

The GO train line that Barbie and I rode was a bit of a micro-society in which our little clique of riders developed into friends. All told there was probably 15 of us at one point that rode together, joked together and on occasion even went out for 'GO train dinners'. Slowly our numbers dwindled through job changes, moving and life in general.

It was one person's move from Ontario to Cape Breton that started the idea of a blog. As a bit of a joke it was suggested creating a blog so that they could keep up with the antics and gaffes that seemed to follow Barbie around.

Through the fine folks at Wordpress I started up the blog *Barbie Fails*. From the beginning the readers were our GO train friends. Slowly co-workers started checking it out. Then we had the growth to social media friends and other Wordpress sites. What shocked me even more was that I started getting messages with stories, which some are here, from people looking to be a part of the blog. This endeavour was beginning to take a life of its own that I was truly shocked at how it did develop.

So I have to thank a few people as well. Aaron, for his contributions with stories from his own GO train that were the future Barbies. Barbie's co-workers who would email me stories of her gaffes at her workplace. My own former co-workers whom I can credit for the stories about engineers and research staff. Rob, who's drive in making short independent movies about things he cares about made me realize that you need to create for what you love not what others want. Anthony, who I witnessed push and strive to have his comic book idea come to life, became an inspiration to not give up on something because someone said no. Lastly my best friend Jeff who has always supported any idea I had no matter how incredibly off the wall.

Colin Brackenridge

Kevin Smith-Michael Moore...separated at birth

Welcome to the wonderful world of *Barbie Fails*. Here will be the great documentation of stories of a real life Barbie and her blonde faux pas in daily life. For the record Barbie is actually a very well educated professional and fairly intelligent person. She's just prone to really silly moments and actions that undermine those facts.

Today during dinner while discussing *Jersey Shore* I mentioned that until this show the most famous Jersey residents that anyone had heard of was Jon Stewart, Bruce Willis, Bruce Springsteen and Kevin Smith. At this moment Barbie-girl piped in with the comment

"Kevin Smith isn't from Jersey. He's Canadian, I saw him in Ontario with his family in the movie *Sicko*"

It was at this moment I clued in she meant Michael Moore and I mentioned that Kevin Smith is the dark haired, bearded guy who made *Clerks, Mallrats, Chasing Amy* you know movies that took place in Jersey and Michael Moore is the documentary movie maker from Detroit with family in Windsor, Ontario and is a little more blondish in colour.

To further hit this point home I opened up the IMDB profiles on both so she could actually see the similarities. This didn't help my cause any.

"Look they both wear glasses and baseball hats. It's an easy screw up", said a defiant Barbie.

"Really? Because the one has a very dark beard and dark hair sticking out of his cap and the other one is definitely much lighter"

In Barbie's final act of defence she did add "Well, they're both fat"

Woodscrews aren't made of wood?

While eating dinner, since this is where most our profound conversations seem to occur, I found the kitten playing with a screw on the floor and picked it up. When discussing where it came from I mentioned how it might have fallen from her nana's old dinner table that she has. In great Barbie fashion she said:

"But this table would only have wood screws"

"Yep, this table should have just wood screws in it", I added.

"So where did this screw come from?"

At this point in time it was crystal clear that she thought wood screws were actually wood. I had to inform my Barbie that wood screws have fine threads with a pointed tip but were still made of metal not wood. She hesitated before adding "I knew that" but her face betrayed her and told me that she thought a wood screw was made of wood and a metal screw was metal.

Bert and Ernie aren't brothers?

Another great intellectual dinner conversation with Barbie as the topic was that an Ontario Liberal MPP was blaming rural "homophobes" for killing a Bill in Queen's Park that would have changed school sex education programs to teach sexual orientation to kids as young as 8 and the methodology of oral and anal sex to kids who were as young as 11. I mentioned that maybe instead of it being "homophobes" why couldn't it possibly be people who just want to let kids be kids and preserve that great sense of innocence that children are supposed to have.

Barbie mentions "No kidding. I mean why do the need to force kids to grow up before they need to? Like Bert and Ernie. Why did they have to be made gay? They lived in the same house and had separate beds like kids do."

"Um, they aren't kids. They were adults living together", I added at this point.

"What? I thought you just didn't see their parents! I figured they were brothers, I mean after all they're both made of felt."

Barbie's Missing Keys

Barbie and I ride the train back and forth to Toronto and without fail she waits until the last second to look for keys to her car. One particular evening, Barbie became rather agitated because she couldn't find her car keys. She was frantically digging through her purse, which was sitting on her lap, cursing away as the keys could not be found. Becoming desperate, she started digging through the roller bag she had for her computer stuff while getting the point of near tears because the elusive car keys could not be found.

Surrendering all hope of being able to drive her car home, she threw her purse down to the ground cursing the day she bought the purse, seeing as she figured that this purse's lack of a zipper to close it was the reason her keys went missing. And then as if some fairy godmother has answered her prayers there lay her keys...in her lap the whole time having been covered by the purse.

Barbie and the Escalator of Doom

It was a calm Tuesday morning in downtown Metropolis when our dear friend, Miss Barbie, decided to add some excitement to the day in a manner that only she could. Upon leaving the concourse of Metro Hall our fine heroine embarked on her journey up the escalator. However her laptop roller bag had other ideas. Since Barbie hadn't paid full attention to the positioning of her bag, which is always about 8 inches over hanging on the right side, she entered the escalator while almost brushing up against the right side rail...this is how it began. The bag, overhanging as normal, caught onto the framework of the escalator and prevented it from moving. Barbie, unaware of this, was jerked backwards a little and proceeded to run down the escalator, which was moving up by the way, reminiscent to that of a treadmill while trying to unhook the bag from its captor. After 5 seconds of this amusing sight, another rider getting ready to ride the escalator unhooked the bag to allow Barbie to finish her trip to work and experience new adventures.

Barbie and the NCAACP

The other week I was having a conversation with our Barbie-girl about a mutual friend that we commute with to Toronto. So I was telling Barbie that our friend's eldest daughter received early acceptance to Trent University and the coach there wanted her to practice with his girls' soccer team. Barbie said at that moment, "Oh did she get a scholarship." I informed Barbie that Canadian universities don't hand out athletic scholarships (most people don't know this actually). At that moment I added "Well, Simon Fraser in B.C. might because they place in the NCAA set up and not CIAU."

It was at that time Barbie had the look in her eyes that let me know something "Barbie-ish" was about to happen.

"I don't understand, what does Simon Fraser have to do with the group for black people", was the comment that accompanied the look.

"Black people?!?!?" was my immediate response and instantly clued in and clarified, "The NCAA is the College Athletics Association. You are thinking of the NAACP which is the National Association for the Advancement of Coloured People."

"Oh, yeah, well they play sports and have a lot of A's so it's an easy mistake", was her rebuttal and saving face comment.

Barbie and the Popcorn Conundrum

So during the Christmas shopping season Barbie was at the local mall with one of her friends. While out shopping the two ladies came across a Kernels to which Barbie said to her friend "Let's go see what samples they have." And so it began...

Barbie proceeds to help herself to a few kernels out of the bucket for her gastronomic enjoyment. After popping these morsels for her enjoyment, Barbie noticed a puzzled look on her friend's face. Finally, her friend blurts out, "Um, I don't think those are samples"

Somewhat perplexed at this, Barbie turns to her friend and notices a lady at the cash register staring at her while holding the bucket of popcorn Barbie had just sampled. Barbie then looked to the other side and noticed the lady's kids staring at her. A few seconds of looking back and forth between the two passed and somewhat embarrassed and unsure of what to say, Barbie says to the lady
"I'm really sorry but I thought it was free samples", and she just smiled, placed the stolen, uneaten kernels into her mouth and high-tailed it out of the mall, leaving the family with a story to share for years.

For the record, the flavour of the day was Cheddar Cheese.

Barbie's Bedtime

One evening, after a hectic, busy day at work, Barbie came home and cracked open her laptop to do some additional work that required finishing to meet deadlines for the morning. So after a good two hour of plugging away Barbie decided enough was enough and it was time to unwind on the couch and watch a little television.

As Criminal Minds opening credits faded to black so did Barbie's consciousness. By first commercial break, around 9.10, I gave Barbie a little shake and told her:
"Hey, you're sleeping. Just go up to bed, I can clean up everything down here"
"No I'm not", Barbie said. "I'm just resting my eyes a little. I really am watching."

So I let it be, and without fail, as the commercials ended so did Barbie's foray in the world of those who are awake and to the land of nod she went. Again I waited for the commercial break, around 9.25, to make another attempt to Miss Barbie.
"OK, you aren't watching at all. You feel right asleep again. Just go to bed and I'll settle up. I can always read or something."
"No, I'm watching the show. What's happened again? And I'm comfortable here."

I just shook my head and dropped the issue. And like the previous two incidents our Barbie girl was in the realm of R.E.M. (maybe dreaming of happy, shiny people...who knows) and the show carried on watching her instead of her watching it. At 10.00 when the episode ended I decided this was the appropriate time to make my third attempt.

"Hey, the episode is over. Let's head upstairs", I said. And this is where it all went wrong...

"STOP PRESSURING ME!!!!" Barbie exclaimed.

Once my laughing subsided, she proceeded to say, "I'm comfy here and I don't want to move. Why are you making me get up? Why can't I stay here?"

"You can, and I can just wake you in the morning when the alarm goes off"

Barbie, I think having finally hit a state of waking conscious and extreme grumpiness, decided that going up to a bed would be better rest than the couch and off she went. Although to be honest it was a mild stomping of annoyance as she went upstairs.

Christmas with Barbie

This Christmas season had some great moments with Barbie.

When talking to Barbie about what she'd like for Christmas I got this answer:

"I'd really like to have a diamond stud fill in my back hole"

Apparently she meant diamond earrings to put in the second hole she has in her ears. Good thing I didn't take that one the wrong way.

While sitting at her mom's on Christmas Eve and watching a newscast from the CTV channel coming out of Vancouver, British Columbia there was another great moment. The newscaster was talking about a housing style popular in Vancouver called "The Vancouver Special". During the newscast the reporter stated that we were going to see a report from 1984 in regards to people complaining about the ugliness of the houses. While this replay was happening Barbie, who obviously wasn't paying attention, made this observation:

"What the hell is with those glasses? Don't people learn from the fashion mistakes of the past? I mean geez those didn't look good in the 80's and are even worse now"
"Um, probably because this is a replay of a report from 1984", replied Barbie's brother

That ended that moment.

Barbie Has Double Vision

One morning, Barbie crawled out of bed to get ready for a doctor's appointment, subscribing to her normal morning routine. Barbie checked the clock... time to get up. She hopped in the shower and began her bathing and grooming routine. Barbie was able to read the shampoo bottle, pluck her eyebrows in the mirror and apply make-up without a hitch. After completing this routine, Barbie popped in a pair of her disposable contact lenses (as she is blind as a bat) and began her trek to the doctor.

On the drive to the doctor, Barbie's eyes felt a little foggy, almost like they were too thick. As she continued to drive, she started to notice some really strange events. As she was blinking her eyes Barbie noticed that suddenly she would see double and then it would blend into one shape. This was somewhat alarming as it had never happened to her before. She didn't pay it too much thought, but proceeded to carried on to her scheduled appointment.

By the time she arrived home, Barbie decided enough was enough and decided to remove her contacts as they were bugging her beyond belief. It was at this moment, Barbie realized her vision issues had a very simple solution. Barbie had fallen asleep with her daily contacts still in her eyes from the night before and instead of removing them when she awoke in the morning, she inserted a new set of contacts on top. Apparently, her miraculous 20/20 morning vision was not so miraculous after all.

British Barbie and the EBay Adventure

Ok, this story deviates from my usual Barbie stories. This was told to me by a friend of the family back in Northern Ireland and when hearing the story our Barbie admitted she could see herself doing this. So, we will now have a British Barbie addition to the blog for today.

British Barbie had discovered the joys of selling and buying from her computer at home by the means of *eBay*. One day she decided to sell a dress that she had purchased some time ago but had never gotten around to wearing it. Having paid £20 (about $32) for it she wasn't too attached to it or upset to see it sold so she listed it on *eBay* for auction. After a few days a sale was agreed upon to the sum of £8 (about $13). So the dress, with the original price tag on it since it was never worn, was packaged and shipped out.

Fast forward a few weeks and while window shopping, if that's the appropriate term, on *eBay* our British Barbie found some clothes she was interested in buying, including a new dress. So she goes forth with the transactions through *eBay* and awaited her new items of fashion. The items finally arrive about a week later and as she opens them up she sees a familiar item...a dress of similar colour and cut to the one just sold. As she pulls it out to further investigate British Barbie sees the price tag still hanging from it - yes, my friends, she purchased the same dress back for a sum of £12 (about $19) and therefore had bought the dress twice for a sum of £32 (about $51).

Barbie's Dog and the Hole Debacle

Well, today after work Barbie and I took her little Sheltie for walk in the field behind the house. Her dog loves to walk in the field because we will generally let her go leash-free. As we went along the trails in the brush, many which have been made by the teenagers on the pocket bikes and four-wheelers, we came upon a man-made jump for the riders. So as we approached this jump, we noticed that there was a large hole, approximately 3-foot by 3-foot and about 2-feet deep. Side-stepping the hole, we called to the dog motioning for her to follow the path around the edge of the hole.

Much like her human mother who suffers from bouts of clumsiness, the poor dog just carried on straight for the hole. As we saw her get closer to the hole, we yelled "No, Chelsea! Over here... wait... not there..."

And then it happened.

The poor dog took her front paws and stepped into the great void, and unlike in Bugs Bunny where the laws of gravity don't apply (because he never studied law according to Bugs), poor little Chelsea went face first into the hole. We heard a dull thud as Chelsea's little snout schmucked against the dirt wall of the hole. Stunned, the poor dog looked at us for a few moments, wondering what had happened and then pondering how to get out back out. After a few failed attempts to get herself out of the hole, she dragged herself out and our little walk continued but not without some great mirth as we recounted the 'hole' debacle with Barbie's dog.

Adventures of Barbie's Friend Christine and the Lost Keys

For those unaware Christie is the name of the first black Barbie doll that was released by Mattel (I had to look that up). The other day as I was in my apartment building moving stuff out I came off the elevator with my cart and saw a lady coming to the door. Thinking I was doing the right thing, I opened the door for her so she wouldn't have to waste time playing with the fob lock (those stupid grey plastic things) and she could just get right into the elevator before it left the parking level.

Christie, as we will call the nice Jamaican lady from here on, scrambled through the door and put her arm up to block the elevator door from closing as she was awaiting her husband who was parking his car. No sooner than she had placed her arm up the cruel lords of fate decided to get their mischief-maker Murphy and his dumb laws involved. Poor Christie dropped her keys and they took one bounce and then went kerplunk down the gap between the elevator and the floor.

Standing aghast she just looked at me and went 'How am I to get those back?'
So I said that maintenance should be able to get them and the office was still open. However, still somewhat shocked at this twist of cruelty, Christie decided to wait for her husband and explain to him.

I wished her luck and went on my way. When I told this story to Barbie she sheepishly admitted that this is one of her biggest fears and could completely see herself doing this.

British Barbie and the Mystification of Multi-tasking

I had forwarded the blog to British Barbie to let her know of her guest spot, and so she could read the whimsical on-goings of our Toronto Barbie. She loved the stories and provided even more material thus ensuring she has a regular spot on this blog site.

So one day our British Barbie was in a bit of a scramble in her house doing laundry and making her morning tea. Of course things never work out as planned when multi-tasking, as most of us can attest to.
On goes the kettle, out comes one load from the washing machine and into the dryer and another load into the washing machine. I should note to our readers that in Britain the laundry machines are often in the kitchen and not in a separate room like over here in North America.
Sure enough the kettle pops and in the scramble of doing all three tasks things start to crumble. British Barbie throws the two tea bags into the washing machine instead of the teapot, the detergent into the dryer instead of the washer and couldn't find the tea bags on the counter so she put instant coffee into her cup and poured the kettle opting for a cup of "joe" instead.
As she started all the machines up and sat to her coffee, the dryer started smoking from the detergent powder getting into the electrical wires. She jumped up to shut the dryer down and pull the clothes out fearing that the burning smell was actually her clothes on fire. Thankfully they weren't but she did need a repair man to come in and take about the entire machine before it could be fixed.
When the washer stopped her load of laundry, and it was a white load, came out a lovely colour of what can only be described as Tetley Tea brown.
Needless to say it was a rather expensive morning for our poor British Barbie.

Barbie's Trip to Bizarro World

Well folks I have to apologise for the lack of activity but to be truthfully honest my blog's inspiration has been rather hazard free...until last week.

In case I haven't mentioned our Barbie likes to figure skate and this past week it was getting ready for the figure skating that started a chain reaction of events that created the material for this posting.

Barbie packed her skating gear into her bag and prepared to leave for practice. As she went to the car, she loaded her bags into the back seat and closed the car door. Barbie then got into the car and got ready to leave with keys in hand, reached out to grab the steering wheel

...and...

She realised she had entered the car on the **passenger side of the car**. After skating Barbie came home, in one piece thankfully (despite getting her foot caught in the bottom of her pants) and got changed out of her skating gear. At this moment Barbie realised that she had been wearing her underwear inside out all day. This lead to quite the exasperated comment of 'Oh Lord. What is going on in my head today?'

At this moment, the trifecta of bizarro world errors occurred. Barbie pulled on her pyjama shorts, and sure enough, she put them on backwards.
This lead the ultimate sigh of defeat and the admission of 'Good God, I just can't get anything right today'

So to keep score here:

1. Entered the car to drive but sat in the passenger side
2. Had underwear on inside out all day
3. Put on pyjama pants backwards

Barbie's New Word

Well, following in the steps of such great linguistic geniuses as Stephen Colbert (*truthiness*), Pat Riley (*three-peat*) and even William Shakespeare (*bedazzled* and *circumstantial*) our Barbie girl has added to the English language with her own word creation.

Last night as we were sitting around watching the new **Shark Week: 20th Anniversary** DVD that I had picked up I noticed that Barbie had turned into Sleeping Beauty, as duly noted in previous blog posts as to what happens when the television is on. As the episode *Shark Attack Survivors* was ending, and the extremely late time of 8.45pm, Barbie stirred a little and said 'Shall we watch another episode?'

I sort of looked cock-eyed at Barbie and went 'Or we just go to bed since you're sleeping already. I can easily read a book.'

'But I'm not sleeping. We can watch another episode', was Barbie's answer.

Again I looked at her rather askew, and went 'Um, your eyes were closed and you missed half the episode.'

'Maybe, but I wasn't sleeping. I was in my ***pre-sleep*** before I go to bed'

Ok, I'll admit that I'm not Mr. Oxford or anything, but even I know that pre-sleep isn't a proper word ... so I called her out on it.
'Pre-sleep? That's not even a word. It's called sleeping or napping. Not pre-sleeping.'

'Well, it should be a word. And I'm going to make it a word!'

So ladies and gentlemen here it is, Barbie's new word and its corresponding definition for the new English word **Pre-sleep**

Pre-sleep - The act of sleeping outside of the bedroom and in no greater than 60 minutes prior to one's bedtime. Pre-sleeping most often occurs on a couch while a television program is broadcasting in the background.

Barbies-In-Training...and this is why I drink

OK, so I get an email from a reader who felt that this deserved a place on the *Barbie Fails Blog,* and after reading his email I fully agree.

"I was sitting on the GO train tonight heading home and two ladies (aged somewhere around 16-18 bracket) were trying to play a game where each girl would name a new animal using the last letter of the animal name used (e.g. goat, next person needs to find a T animal).
During the announcements at one station I couldn't hear what one of the girls says, but the next answer is *beef cow*. The other girl challenges the answer with get vigor saying that there is no such thing as a *beef cow.* At this moment I had a small snicker and felt badly for the, what I thought was, lesser intelligent of the two girls. That moment of grandeur was short-lived and the intellectual bubble was not just burst but mushroom clouded when she felt the need to add the following "and the **REAL** answer is *steak cow"*. They fight about this for the next 5 minutes.
At the end of all this they came to the conclusion and belief that there was a difference between the 2 animals - *beef and steak cows*......this is why I cry for the future."

And it is for reasons like this that I drink...in fact I might have one now

British Barbie and the Passport

Well here is another adventure from our overseas Barbie and her contributions to our blog.

British Barbie was taking a vacation with her sister and had her son, Colin, take the two of them to the airport. Before leaving British Barbie double checked her purse to make sure that her passport was in on her. On the way to the airport her son stopped to let British Barbie mail some letters. British Barbie and her sister arrived at the airport and queued up to check in. All of a sudden there was no passport. Since she had double checked her purse before leaving she was adamant that the passport must have fallen out at the x-ray machine that all bags go through now. So off goes British Barbie to check with security. They can't find the passport. Since our British Barbie was insistent on the passport having been in her purse she was able to persuade the fine security staff at the airport actually opened up and dismantled the casings of the x-ray machine in case it fell inside. Alas, it was not to be found.
The next logical solution was that our friend British Barbie must have dropped it as she was getting out of her son's car. Since it was 11.30pm and pitch black outside, our ever persuasive British Barbie managed to get the airport police to patrol the entranceway with their flashlights on and going up and down the road with such determination that you would have thought it was a crime scene investigation. In the middle of all this British Barbie's cell phone rang and it was her brother-in-law, Alan, calling.

Turns out that British Barbie dropped her passport while at the post box delivering letters. A girl walking home found it, picked it up and called the emergency contact number on it. That number happened to be British Barbie's mum. Her mum then called the Alan at work. Alan met the girl who had found the passport and then rang Colin. Colin was halfway home from the airport at this time so Alan flew off in his car, met Colin along the way and Colin drove off like Formula One driver Eddie Irvine back to the airport. British Barbie met him outside the doors and with just minutes to spare managed to get onto her flight. Upon boarding the plane British Barbie and her sister were met with a round of applause from both the stewardesses and the passengers since the adventures of the missing passport apparently had been told to them to explain what was happening with the two 'missing' passengers.

Engineering Barbie and the Camping Gear

This blog started out as the adventures of one particular person who we nicknamed Barbie and whom, on occasion, did or said silly things that made you slap your forehead. Well, first we expanded to stories of a family friend that we nicknamed British Barbie. Then we had the Barbie-in-training story and now, courtesy of my workplace, we have Engineering Barbie.

Today while walking through the corridors of work to go and get beverages for our afternoon break the two co-workers who were with me started talking about an upcoming camping trip. During this discussion it was bandied around on who was bringing what. I, somewhat jokingly, said to my male colleague that all he needed to bring was beer. Engineering Barbie then told me that wasn't allowed because you can't bring glass onto the campsite. So, not to be out done, I said "that's fine, they sell beer in cans too".
"No, you can't bring cans either. No glass, no cans are allowed. You must bring it in a non-throw-away-able container"

I have to admit I stood there gobsmacked and said "Did you just say non-throw-away-able?"

Sheepishly she admitted that she had. I then asked "Don't you mean re-usable or non-disposable?"

Again she sheepishly admitted that was exactly what she meant but couldn't think of the word. And then in a moment of defiance she said "Well, I'm tired and not thinking straight. That's why I'm going for coffee"

Barbie Needs Facial Recognition Programming

Today while driving home from the train station Barbie started telling me about the trip to the book store that she had taken with a co-worker. While at the bookstore Barbie stumbled across the hot selling pseudo children's book "*Go The F**k To Sleep*" by Adam Mansbach. So I mention that I had heard of this book and on YouTube there is an audio reading of the book by Samuel L. Jackson and it was hilarious.

We then started talking about other things that had happened that day and then Barbie goes "I can't wait to get home and listen to Morgan Freeman read the story".

I openly admit that I took that same look that your pet dog has when confused, yep the one where you sort of cock your head to one side while looking completely stunned and thinking "WHAT?!?!?!?" However, I managed to stay composed enough to ask "Don't you mean Samuel L. Jackson?"

"Uh?" was the immediate response and followed with, "Well, they both have gravelly voices"

"No they don't, in fact they sound very different. Jackson has a gravelly voice but Freeman doesn't", was my retort back.

"Yeah they do....don't they? Well they are both black! And they both do voice over work!" and at that moment the lights came on and even Barbie knew that another Barbie moment had been created.

"Both black? Yeah but distinctly different sounding and looking people! However it would be funny if they had that other guy read it out, damn what's his name, you know Darth Vader! The guy who did the voice over for CNN, you know 'This is CNN'."

"You mean Dick Butkus?"

"Dick Butkus? He's a big, scary white dude", I replied.

"Oh. Well I guess that wouldn't be right...but he has a gravelly voice right?"

I had to concede that Dick Butkus does have a gravelly voice. At this time we pulled into the gas station and Barbie started to fill her car up. As she began she opened the back door up and goes "Luther Vandross!"

I looked over and went "Luther Vandross, while black, most certainly does not have a deep voice and never voiced over anything."

So she closed the door and finished filling up the gas tank while I sat there pondering in my head on the name that eluded me. As she gets into the car and ready to drive away she gives it one more stab and goes "Craig T. Nelson"

I shook my head and went "No. He's a white guy too"

"Well he has one of those threesie style names! You know *yadda yadda yadda.*"

"Yes he does", and in a moment of clarity I remembered who it was and said, "but it's James Earl Jones. However since you knew it was a triple shot name how in earth did you come out with Luther Vandross?"

Somewhat sheepishly she replied "Well it has lots of syllables"

I will admit, in her defense, she hasn't slept well in the last 2 nights which tends to create these moments we enjoy. However this isn't the first time that she hasn't confused faces if you remember the Michael Moore/Kevin Smith moment of 'They are both fat' or the Bert/Ernie moment of 'They are both made of felt'.

Listen up Peak Freans, Barbie says they aren't Nice

While watching the TV last night Barbie and I were having a cup of tea and we brought out a box of *Peek Freans Assorted Tea Biscuits*. As Barbie was eating one of the cookies she developed a look of disgust that one develops when something putrid enters your mouth.

"This cookies says 'Nice' on it", Barbie exclaimed. "It's a lie there nothing nice about this taste"

At this point I was going to bring up that the Nice is actually a reference to the town in France where Peek Freans is from however Barbie cut me off with

"Oh, wait, it might mean Nice (pronounced Niece)." Barbie realised.

"Yeah, it's named after the town in France. Peek Freans used to have that as their advert that 'they aren't nice but Nice (niece)'."

Barbie looked at me and went "Well, it says nice and it should say crap because that's what they taste like"

After a few seconds past Barbie looked backed over at me and went "You're going to write this one aren't you?"

"Absolutely" I said.

Teen Barbies and the Food They Like

Another great story from a follower who reads the blog in regards to the silliness he's overheard on his commuter train from *Teen Barbies* or *Barbies-in-Training*.

It seems these young ladies, 3 in total, were riding the GO train into Toronto and discussing food options they enjoy. Based on the story told to me it went something like this:

"I really enjoy certain seafood, like crab and stuff. And I absolutely love shrimp", says teen #1.

"No, I'm not a fan of that stuff", retorts teen #2. "I'm more a beef girl."

"Yeah, I don't really like beef", replies teen #1.

"Well, growing up my dad and granddad used to go splits on half a cow", explains teen #2. "So we wound up with a lot of beef and all the different cuts of beef in our freezer."

"Oh wow, that would be nice. The different steaks and hamburgers and stuff", chipped in teen #3.

At this moment it all went downhill as teen #1 added, "Oh that is cool. Did you get bacon with that too?"

Teen #2 replies "Yeah I think we did. I always had bacon in the house so I guess bacon does come with it"

Apparently a few moments passed when all of a sudden one of those scientific miracles, like the Big Bang, occurred on the train and teen #3 had a great moment of clarity (or at least the connection of another synapse) and she piped up "Um, I don't think bacon comes from a cow...I think bacon comes from pigs"

The three girls dropped the conversation at that point, probably due to the confusion they were all feeling due to such a monumental step in intellect.

Barbie's Brother Learns about Genealogy

The other day we were out at Pizza Hut getting dinner and Barbie's brother was with us. In honour of the actual Barbie doll's family we'll call him Todd since this was the name given to the figure who was made as Barbie's younger brother from 1965-71 (thanks to Google and Wikipedia for that).

So for those you who don't know Todd, he's a bit of a smartarse and likes to make one-line comments to get a reaction from people - a heat seeker if you will. So as we are sitting at the table with our food Todd makes the remark to Barbie, and one that cuts all women to the bone, of:
"Take it easy on the food before your ass gets too big to fit through the door"

Now, having been the witness to many of these comments and verbal jarring between the two siblings, my immediate thought was that Barbie was going to reach across the table smack her brother and call him one of many names ranging from 'jerk' to 'asshole'. But that is not what happened. Instead Barbie's retort was:
"Well I'm eating for two now"

Well Todd's jaw dropped quicker than when Phil 'The Drill' Williams recorded the fastest knockout in boxing history over Brandon Burke. And for the first time ever Todd was caught speechless. After about 30 seconds of the awkward silence from her brother Barbie confessed that she's not pregnant and we carried on with the meal.

Fast forward 24 hours to the next day and Todd comes by Barbie's house to hang out and drink some beers. Instantly the ribbing starts when he begins bugging Barbie about the 'pregnancy gag' by telling her:
"Well, I think you need to cut back on the junk food and eat healthier for little Todd Jr"

I stood there looking at him like I had misheard what was said. Slowly I added

"You do realise the for the baby, if there was one, to be Todd Jr means that you, Todd, would have to be the father then?"

Todd stood there looking like a deer in headlights as you could see the gears in his head working triple speed and trying to remember his Grade 10 biology lesson about Gregor Mendel and the peas.

"Oh. Yeah that would be weird and completely trailer park. Do you think you can at least put Todd in his name then?"

So I think for Christmas I might have to buy Todd the following book: *The Complete Idiot's Guide to Genealogy*

Stationary? Or Missionary?

The adventures continue...but with Barbie's friend today. Barbie's friend, Tracy, with having a bit of romance with her husband Todd.
While enjoying some 'marital relations' Tracy developed a bit of a muscle cramp. Trooping on she fought her way through it for a while but eventually the coitus related injury became too sore and Tracy needed to switch things around from the position they were in.

So Tracy, meaning well, told Todd "I'm starting to cramp a little here, can we switch over to the stationary position?"
Todd, admittedly confused, asked "Stationary or missionary? I know the latter but not so much the other one unless you just plan on not moving at all during this."

Barbie-In-Training: It Only Charges When You Plug It into the Wall

Yesterday I received an email from a friend, and fellow train rider, about a *Barbie-ish* style faux pas that she herself committed. Below is the context of the email from Steffie (thanks again for the list of Barbie friends Wikipedia):

Yesterday morning I grabbed my cell phone off the charger as I was running out the door to catch my train.

When I arrived at work I noticed my battery was still at only 1/2 power....I said to my co-workers that this is not the first time I had charged my phone over the last week and then noticed that the battery was not fully charged.....

 I got all kinds of advice about this, because it seems everyone is an expert when it comes to electronics or medical remedies:

"You should let the battery drain and then charge it, it will help prolong the battery life"

"You should take out the battery and make sure there is no dirt around it" - I tried to get the battery out.......no luck.....I could not even get the back of the phone off!!!!

 So when I arrived home last night I plugged the cell phone into the charger and nothing showed on the screen to say it was charging....so I unplugged it and plugged it in again, still nothing...so I unplugged it and plugged it in again, still nothing..............Then I noticed the other end of the charger was not plugged into the wall.

In the title of the email it was stated "Does this qualify me for the blog?"...and the answer is yes, yes it does.

Musical Genius? Ludwig Von Barbie you are not...

Last night Barbie's brother popped over and asked if we wanted to go to Dairy Queen as he had been introduced to a float from Dairy Queen. He has had floats, in the sense that we are thinking with ice cream and your favourite soft drink, but this was something different and you have to specify it to the cashier as it's not on the menu.

However, that's not the crux of this story. As we were driving and listening to music in the truck a country song came on, and I admit country is one of my least favourite music flavours, so I asked "Can we get something else playing?", especially in light of the fact that just before it was a rock song so I know he has a rather varied taste of music on his iPod.

"Yeah, no problem", he says. Then upon flipping to the next song he asked, "How's this one?"

Credence Clearwater Revival's version of *I Heard It through the Grapevine* came on. This I was good with, although I will admit I prefer the Marvin Gaye version best. So as the song was playing, and it was all of 30 or 40 seconds old, Barbie's brother turns to her and asks, as an apparent jab at her preference for Top 40 music:
"Do you know who this is?"

And with great conviction and certainty she proclaimed "Yes I do!"

I thought this was great as I enjoy listening to CCR and the fact that she knew who it was meant I could play the odd song in the car during trips then...or so I thought.

"This is the California Raisins! So yes I know who it is."

I think instead of mentally imagining myself slapping my forehead, I actually physically did slap it this time.

"No, this is not the California Raisins. This is CCR - Credence Clearwater Revival. The version you're thinking of was done as a commercial with dancing raisins and using Marvin Gaye's version of the song", I told her. "This is the same song, but different version all together"

"Oooohhhh!!!! So the California Raisins weren't a real group?" she asked.

"No, they were Claymation raisins dancing about the screen like a Motown revival act", I told her.

She thought for a second and then with great pride said "Yeah, but at least I knew that they sang this at some point"

Holiday Befuddlements Part One

Well Happy Thanksgiving to my Canadian readers. Being a family holiday I figured I'd share a story of holiday confusion that is well suited to this blog and the stories on it. Unfortunately, this isn't a story of our friend Barbie but rather about my 12-year-old son. These stories took place when he was 10 but are funny none the less.

This story takes place at Christmas right after my son made his way downstairs to see the bounty left by Santa. The entertainment centre was wrapped in Christmas wrapping to hide the new Nintendo Wii that was hooked up to the television by Santa himself. As the young lad entered into the room I said to him, "Right, start with any gift you want"

He looked around the room with that scanning radar that all young kids have when it comes to gifts and then went straight to his stocking. I let this go since, by tradition, we had always started with stocking in our house. Once the stocking was done, and probably some mental maths on when he'd get to eat what chocolates he got, he began the scan of the room again.

Now, knowing myself as a child, I expected the biggest gift with his name on it to be the one that he made a beeline to and started ripping open like a frenzied shark. So the biggest gift in the room was quite simply the wrapped up entertainment unit. However, he went to the tree and pulled one of the smaller packages. To say I was confused would be an understatement. So he opens this one and then goes off to the tree again and selects another one. At this point I'm looking around the room for either a hidden camera in case the show *Candid Camera* was making a re-appearance or for the sight of Rod Serling in case my house was being used for an episode of *Twilight Zone*.

By gift number three I looked at my son and with a tone of confusion "Don't you want to open the big gift right here" and I pointed at the entertainment centre. With the eyes gazing widely, he made his way to the entertainment centre and ripped open the paper around it.

To set the scene here, there was a Wii wired up to the television and sitting beside it. On top of the television was the remote controllers. So here's what ensued after the paper was shredded off the unit:

"Oh sweet!!!"

I figured Santa had hit the golden egg for gifts for my son that year...and then it was followed with:

"Santa gave me a Wii remote that I can take to Granny's"

To say I was somewhat confused is an understatement. How is it that he saw the remote and not the big white block beside the television?

So I mention "Um, what about the thing beside the TV?"

He takes a look and with big eyes exclaims "NICE!!! Santa got us a Wii and he hooked it up already. Man, he must really like us"

So to this day I haven't figured out why my child went for the smaller gifts, or how after opening such a big gift he missed seeing the Wii beside the television and lastly how he thought that only a Wii remote would show up without the Wii but still required an entire entertainment unit to be wrapped up. If I ever do sort this out I am asking for my Ph.D. is psychology.

Holiday Befuddlements Part Two

Well, the second installment of holiday guffaws starring none other than my son...again! He apparently doesn't do holidays so well.

So about a year and a half ago on Easter Sunday my son made his way downstairs when awoke and plopped himself on the couch. In walking down the stairs from his room he must have passed at least 3 small chocolate Easter Eggs that were left by the Easter Bunny, and he hadn't noticed. However, he did remember there were hockey games on the night before and he flipped on one of the sports channels to see the highlights and scores.

As he was sitting there I turned to him and said "Hey, what day is today?"

"Sunday"

"What Sunday?"

"Um, Easter Sunday?" he answered with a little uncertainty.

"And what happens on Easter Sunday?"

"We go to Granny's for dinner?", again with some uncertainty.

"Yes, but what else happens on Easter Sunday?"

He sat there for a little while and pondered the question for a while and then answered, with great confidence, "I know. Jesus rose from the dead"

Now, I couldn't fault him in this answer because he was technically right. So I said "Yes that bit is also right. However, that's not what I was getting at. Who comes on Easter Sunday?"

I would be lying if I said he answered right away, but to be honest it took the better part of a minute before he muttered to me "The Easter Bunny comes on Easter"

"Yes the Easter Bunny comes and does what?"

At that moment another synapse connected and he exclaimed "Oh man, I have chocolate eggs to find"

And he ran off on his little hunt while I sat there wondering once again how my offspring's mind works.

School's For Fools

So this little Barbie fail took place today on the way home from work and featured our lovely Barbie herself.

While driving home tonight from the train we passed a man combing his dog in the garage and I mentioned it because this dog was HUGE!!!!!

So as we drive by I say to Barbie, "Hey that guy had his dog on a stool and brushing it."

"What kind of dog was it?" asked Barbie. And as I said it was massive and I had no clue what kind of dog it was...after all I am not Cesar Milan.

"No idea but it was massive. Looked like a bloody black bear sitting there in the garage."

Then Barbie chimes in, "Oh, that reminds me, what's her name on the train said what kind of shepherd she had but I forgot."

"You mean Charlene?"

"Yeah, her. But do you remember what kind of shepherd was it? I keep thinking Alsatian but you told me that word so it can't be that." answers Barbie.

"She has a Belgian Shepherd. An Alsatian is a German Shepherd in Britain."

And then the golden moment we are all waiting for, "Ok you have to stop teaching me stuff, it's confusing me! My brain is obviously full as I'm forgetting things."

And on that note ladies and gentlemen I have been officially told that you can have too much learning.

Barbie's Blackberry and the Cloak of Invisibility

The other day Barbie was in a meeting with her fellow co-workers and a tragic event occurred - she misplaced her Blackberry.

Now for anyone who has a Blackberry, whether it be for business or personal, knows that these devices have been nicknamed 'Crackberry' for a reason. The device is an addiction with its ability to send you emails, text messages and BBM's. But at least it's not the type of addiction that has you dancing on tables topless or sleeping in cardboard box.

OK, back to the story, Barbie misplaced her Blackberry. As she was packing up after the meeting she slowly realized that her Blackberry had become undone from her pants and had dropped somewhere. The big question was where?
Placing on her proverbial Sherlock Holmes cap the search began. Barbie started her search. She searched her purse, her laptop roller-bag, the table and all around the meeting room in general. Alas there was no success in her search.

At this point Barbie's co-worker, Lori, came into the meeting room and asked her what the problem was. Barbie informed Lori that she had lost her Blackberry during the meeting and couldn't find it. Lori came up with the idea that they should call Barbie's Blackberry. This seemed to be an agreed upon method. So Lori went out to the hallway and started calling from her Blackberry, however Barbie also started calling from the meeting room conference phone. Needless to say there was nothing but a busy signal to be heard. Lori noticed that Barbie had also been calling and decided that the plan should be that she would call Barbie's Blackberry from her own Blackberry and they could trace the sound and locate the missing device. So, Lori calls the Blackberry and the ringing begins. So the audio bloodhound work begins. As each ring occurs the two ladies close in on the 'sounds of music' from Barbie's Blackberry much like Tommy Lee Jones on Harrison Ford in 'The Fugitive'.
Barbie finally nailed down the location of the sounds and found her Blackberry...underneath her scarf on her seat. Yes, it seems the

Blackberry had come undone from Barbie's pants, and slid underneath her scarf. So poor Barbie had actually been sitting on the phone which, in her somewhat defense, had been hidden by her scarf much like Harry Potter and his Cloak of Invisibility.

Imagine if someone called the phone and it started vibrating while she was sitting on it?

Engineering Ken and the Hole Issues

As some of you know I work with a lot of engineers. Many of them are supposed to be very smart individuals as they are pursuing their Master's and Ph.D.'s in their respective fields of studies. However, these people can generate some of the best 'Barbie Fail' moments that even has Barbie herself shake her head in disbelief.

Yesterday I was eating lunch in my office with two co-workers when Engineering Ken, who just obtained his Master's Degree, came skulking into the workshop with a rather embarrassed look about him. He wandered into my office area and stopped at the doorway.

"Can I ask you something?" he asked.

"Sure what do you need", I replied.

"How can I get this off?" he asked. At that moment he raised his left hand up and sitting on his baby finger was a gear belt cog.

I have to admit I wanted to laugh, and laugh hard. However, I could see that he was really embarrassed by this so I bit my tongue...really, really, really hard.

"Here you can try this", I said as I tossed him a small bottle of Vaseline I keep for greasing some parts up. Engineering Ken looked perplexed at this and was wondering how he would fit his finger into the small jar deep enough to loosen the cog from his knuckle. It seems, that despite knowing the algorithms for force and stress, our poor friend couldn't muster the idea of using his other hand to take some of the petroleum jelly and apply it to his knuckle.

Seeing this struggle with the concept of how to apply Vaseline I offered him another solution. "Or you can go spray some WD-40 on it"

So, like a mouse, he scurried off to find the WD-40. About 20 seconds later he went walking, rather briskly, past the office.

"Did it work?" I called out.

Without even looking back "Yes. Thanks"

"Can I bring this up as events of interest at Thursday's team meeting?" I asked mildly joking (ok not really joking).

"Um, I would prefer you didn't". At that moment he dropped his head and scurried out of the workshop with pace worthy of an Olympic track star.

I have to be honest, my two co-workers and I absolutely killed ourselves laughing when he left.

Bay Street Banker Ken and Busboy Ken Might Combine For Triple Digit IQ

The first story I heard today on the GO train as Barbie and I were traveling into work. So sitting in the four seats ahead of us were four guys who work in the Bay Street area of Toronto. One of them told this story of what happened to him on Friday after work:

Banker #1 "So you guys should hear what happened to me this weekend"

Banker #2 "Why what happened?"

Banker #1 "Well, we start pulling into Georgetown and I realize I can't find my car. I'm looking everywhere and then I realize I drove into work that morning"

Banker #3 "No. How much did that cost you?"

Banker #1 "It cost a lot. First I had to cab it home and get my kid ready for his hockey. Then we had to cab it to the arena and home. When my wife came back later that night I had to get her to drive me downtown to get the car. And of course I had exceeded the time limits for early bird parking and had to pay regular rates which were huge. Man, I'm never going to do that again"

At this point the four men laughed and got off the train but I have the sneaking suspicion that it's not the first time he's done this and that his three friends have probably done it at least once as well.

Story number two comes from my sister who works in a restaurant in Kitchener. She sent me the following email.

Our busboy goes into the fridge (not big 10' x 4' at most) looks around and then says to me when I opened the door

"Where's the ice?"

I had to shake my head and then pointed to the stand-up freezer that is right beside the walk-in fridge.
He's a 5th year student in high school.....scary if he is our future.

Barbie and the Reservation

As I have mentioned in previous blog postings Barbie and I ride the GO train into Toronto for our jobs. When you ride with the same people day in and day out for 5 years, in my case and 3 years in Barbie's case, you get to develop what is referred to as 'train friends'. Our case is a little different as we have evolved our friendships with our 'train friends' into just regular friends. We have meals with them, invite them to social gatherings, and have celebrated retirements, weddings and child births as well as mourned deaths. To sum it up, we just keep in touch with each other on a basis much more than just commuters sharing a ride into the city.

So last night was one of our 'GO train gatherings' as we had dinner at Kelsey's in Brampton - which by the way the service is horrid. We will have to seriously look at a new dinner venue. So taking the train home last night there were four of us sitting together having a good old chat. During this chat the familiar tones of the theme from *The Twilight Zone* could be heard as Rod Serling voice overlaid his monologue that began each show. Yes it was time for our loving Barbie to exit from reality have a 'moment'.

"Did you make a reservation?" she asked of me. And since we had 12 people coming it was a valid question but I was in a smart arse mood.

"Do I look Native American to you?" I replied sarcastically.

Instantly the other two ladies with us started snickering. It became obvious that a joke had occurred and that poor Barbie missed it. With a look of confusion she said,
"I don't get it."

"Ok", I said. "Where do natives live?"
I was fully expecting at this point the conversation would end as Barbie would then clue into my reservation reference. Especially since she

garnered that look of confidence she gets whenever she has the impression that she knows the answer 100%.

"In a tepee" she adamantly exclaims.

"Oh, Jesus Christ", I muttered. "Ok, and where is the tepee located?" This time I was really sure she would get the answer required.

With great certainty, but not the overbearing confidence she had with answer one, she answered,
"In Wawa."

Fighting the urge to slap my forehead like one of the Three Stooges I gathered the patience for one more hinting question.

"And that big piece of land in Wawa is called what?" I asked while making hand gestures to show obvious acreage of land.

She looked as us a little befuddled and answered, really unsure of herself, "A reserve?!?!?"

"A reservation. Get it now?"

"Yes", she said with annoyance. "But I don't think it's really all that funny you know. I've actually seen them living in tepees in Wawa so I really wasn't wrong", she proclaimed with great defiance at our humour.

Engineering Barbie Might Be Dyslexic...so she thinks

OK so I was sitting in the office having lunch with Industrial Designer Ken and Engineering Barbie. The topic of conversation was the tours we had going on and the 'big media' one that we have coming up. During this I mention that I found a new shirt that said the following:

I'm drunk
You're ugly
And tomorrow I'll be sober

We all got a good chuckle out of it and I then stated "Maybe I'll start wearing it to the team meetings. Or maybe I'll dig out my good old *'I'll try being nicer if you try being smarter'* shirt that I have."

"You didn't wear a shirt like that to team meeting did you?" asked Industrial Designer Ken.

"Absolutely I did. I mean it's not like they'll let me wear my hat that says 'G.F.Y.'"

Engineering Barbie had a good snicker over this but Industrial Designer Ken looked a little lost.

"I don't get it. What does G.F.Y stand for?"

"It means Go F*** Yourself", I replied.

Engineering Barbie then looked perplexed and went "I thought it meant Jesus F***ing Christ"

I then looked at Engineering Barbie and went "You do realize that would be JFC not GFY right?"

In her best attempts to cover her tracks she answered back with "Maybe I'm dyslexic"

"Um, dyslexia means you scramble letters up...not create whole new letters", I told her.

Undeterred she answered back with that classic reply, 'Whatever". And off she went leaving both Designer Ken and I completely confused and perplexed.

Barbie and the Terry-cloth Kilt

On Sunday things seemed rather uneventful at the Barbie-cave. She was going out to go visit her Nana, I was sitting around doing chores and helping my kid with his homework assignment. There just seemed to be a nice air of tranquility due to a lack of unexpected mayhem that generally leads to the creation of stories for the blog.

That lasted until Barbie came home. She asked how far I had gotten in the laundry and I told her that whites were done and one load of blacks. The second load of blacks were in the dryer and first load of colours were in the wash.
"Why?" I asked.
"I spilt my tea on my jeans and sweater", she replied. "I hadn't even left the street when I spilt it all over me."

I started snickering because the sweater, being white, is one that has been victim to a few spills in the last couple of months and I will admit that not all of them were Barbie's fault. So downstairs she went to go spray stain remover on her sweater to try to remove the stains. While down there she decided she'd just throw her jeans in the wash since colours had just begun their cycle. The jeans came off and tossed into the machine. Barbie started rifling through the blacks looking for pants, which given that almost all her work pants are black it was a good gamble. However, I had made sure that the working clothes were washed and dried first so there was none to be found.

Panic begins to develop in Barbie as she now realizes that all she has on is her t-shirt and underwear. Due to the layout of the house the odds of her being able to get up the stairs from the basement, walk past us sitting in the main living room and then up the next set of stairs to the bedroom to get pants and not be noticed were really not looking so favourably. So she starts to dig around the articles that just came out of the dryer. She found herself a nice big towel and quickly fashioned a skirt from it. To ensure that gravity didn't mess with her plans Barbie then took her belt that was on her jeans and fastened it around the waist. At this point she marched herself up the stairs.

Upon hitting the stairs to go up to the bedrooms I noticed the rather odd attire that was being fashioned about the house.

"Trying out for a remake of Braveheart?" I smartly asked since it looked like a kilt. Barbie then regaled us with the story of what had happened. My son and I wasted no time killing ourselves in laughter as our Barbie defiantly marched herself up the stairs to get a proper pair of pants.

Barbie's Hug Machine

The other day as we were sitting watching television little Miss Barbie was fighting sleep, and we've already covered her television-sleep issues in the *Pre-Sleep* article. A rather groggy Barbie looks over at me and goes

"Can I have a hug?"

My first reaction, because I wasn't really paying attention, was "What?"

"I need a hug. So give me a hug or get one of those hug machines", Barbie replies.

"Hug machines? What are you on about?" I asked her.

"You know those hug machines that Shooter McGavin built", Barbie stated.

"Shooter McGavin? The guy from Happy Gilmore? He didn't build a hug machine", was my retort.

"No, the autistic girl with the movie", she replied.

"Temple Grandin?" I asked.

"Yeah that's the one."

"But you said Shooter McGavin. That's not even the right sex never mind the real person/fictional person debate", I said.

"Whatever, their names are close enough. Can I have the hug or not?"

Barbie and the Freudian slip

Last night, as we were watching Netflix, I had made some nice hot chocolate using white chocolate powder and warm milk. As I was bringing the cups out I noticed that my kid had left the foil wrappers from his Hersey's Kisses on the carpet. A little annoyed at the fact he didn't dispose of his trash, and more annoyed that he had knocked it on the floor from the table, I said to him:

"Hey, if you can't throw out your garbage then there'll be no more Hersey Kisses for you! Got it kiddo?"

"Yes dad", he agreed in that great voice that pre-teens use. You know the one that makes you want to give them a high five...to the face!

So we went about drinking our hot chocolate, watching the movie *Daddy Day Care* on Netflix and eating such healthy treats as Kisses, cakes and Reese's Peanut butter Trees (like the cups but tree shaped for Christmas). When we all finished up our drinks and snacks, I decided I'd clean up the dishes. As I was getting the cups and heading to the kitchen I noticed that I had left a wrapper for one of the Reese's trees on the table. As I had only travelled about 5 steps, I backed up and picked up the wrapper to dispose of in the garbage as I made my way into the kitchen.

At that moment Barbie, thinking she'd be a smart arse, looked at me and said mockingly "If you don't put your wrappers in the garbage there'll be no more Reese's Penis for you".

Everything stopped, my son and I both turned and looked at Barbie. The look on her face betrayed the fact that she knew she had made a huge slip up. "I just did it again, didn't I? I said penis instead of pieces", she said. Without even answering her we all just started laughing our heads off.

Please note that she said again!

Barbie Needs an E-Z Bake...or some Oven Mitts

Last week Miss Barbie decided she would make some oatmeal chocolate chip muffins. Given that we don't have a lot of time with the commute from downtown I will admit that we use *Quaker Oats* pre-mix, since the time for making baked goods from scratch just isn't there during the week.

So Barbie mixed everything up, took out the muffin tray and rested it on top of the stove while turning the oven on to warm up. Once she is done with the mix she poured it into the muffin tray, which she has outfitted with the little paper muffin cups. After all this she opened the oven door up and reached for the tray. That was when I heard a loud smash and the scream of "OWWWW".

I went racing into the kitchen and asked what happened. "I burnt my hand", Barbie exclaimed. "I grabbed the pan and one side was fine but the other side was hot".

I surveyed the potential damage, which was minimal. The muffin tray I noticed had three muffins sitting at an odd angle and muffin mix was sitting all over the handles of the pan.

"Where was the pan?" I asked.
"Sitting on top of the stove", Barbie said. "I don't know how it got so hot. Maybe the stove is broken?"
"No, the heat ups up through the rings so they get a little warm even when they aren't on." I told her.

I then took a spoon, tried to straighten up the cups and feed as much of the mixture back into them. Needless to say we had three muffins that resembled the Leaning Tower of Pisa and 9 muffins that were perfectly fine. Barbie also learnt that never touch a pan sitting on the stove with the oven on unless you're wearing oven mitts.

Baking Disaster Turned Good

About 7 or 8 years ago, our dear Barbie had a near baking disaster. During her first years at her job there was a baking event and she had agreed to take part. At the time she was still living with her dad and therefore shared the house with a few folks. This often resulted in a scenario where the left hand didn't always know what the right hand was doing.

So Barbie turned the oven on to pre-heat it for cookies and muffins that she was going to make for the bake sale. Well, it seems that during the baby shower that was hosted at the house the week previous had some left over items such as plates, cups and such. Well it turns out that in the oven, due to a lack of cupboard space, Barbie's step-mom had placed a package of Styrofoam cups. Unbeknownst to Barbie these cups were sitting on a pan in the oven while she was getting her ingredients ready.

A few minutes later Barbie had her prep work done and was ready to bake like Betty Crocker. She opened the oven door to get ready to place her cookie trays and muffin pans in and what should befall her eyes? Yes, there were the Styrofoam cups had been baked and shrunk - sort of like the head of the guy at the end of Beetlejuice.

Fast forward to today. Barbie's place of employment had a tree for which they were encouraged to bring decorations to hang on it. There was going to be a prize for the best ornament on the tree. This weekend, while assembling our own Christmas tree, Barbie found her shrunken cups. She decided that she would take her cups into work and hang them on the tree. Today she was awarded the prize for best decoration. Who would have known that doing a 'Barbie' would come out to be a benefit?

Barbie and the Garden of Eden

On Friday, as we got off the GO Train and were walking to our respective places of employment, Barbie, another train friend and myself were discussing Christmas functions in the office. During this discussion it was mentioned how last year Barbie's brother had attended the play *Joseph and the Amazing Technicolour Dreamcoat* at Stage West in Mississauga. We talked about how Barbie's brother had to have it explained to him that there were two Joseph's in the Bible - Joseph, with his coat of many colours, and Joseph, Jesus' dad. I never mentioned Joseph of Arimathea to him to save on the confusion of a third Joseph.

At this point Barbie explained, "I went to nursery school once, but told my mom that it was silly and I saw no point in colouring in apples."

I looked over at Barbie and asked, "Nursery school? Are you sure it wasn't Sunday school?"

"Oh yeah, it was Sunday school", Barbie said. "But both were held in the church. Anyways I still think colouring an apple was stupid."

"Well, the colouring of the apple would have been the simple lead in for the story of the Eve, the apple and how she tricked..."

Barbie interrupted here with one of her outstanding Barbie-isms "Oh, Johnny Appleseed right?"

"WHAT!!! Johnny Appleseed? No, Adam. The story of Adam, Eve, the serpent and the apple from the Tree of Knowledge. You know the forbidden fruit that got them kicked out of Eden?" I retorted back.

"Um, no I don't think I know that one", said Barbie. "So who is Johnny Appleseed then?"

"American frontiersman. Went around the country planting apple seeds to introduce apples to America." I told her.

"Didn't they already have apples in America?" she asked.

"In areas but he took it to areas that didn't have apples."

"Oh, so what the apple and Eve thing?" Barbie asked.

"When God created man and woman they lived in the Garden of Eden. The devil, in the disguise of a snake, told Eve that she should take an apple from the Tree of Knowledge and feed it to Adam. Eve questioned it but the snake told her that God didn't want them to eat the apple because it would make them Gods. They ate the apple and realized they were naked and covered up."

"Oh this is the whole fig leaf thing right?" Barbie asked.

"Yep. Anyways, God saw them covering up and asked why. They mentioned their nakedness shamed them. So for violating his order God banished them from the Garden of Eden."

"Ohhhh", said Barbie. "So Johnny Appleseed really had nothing to do with it at all then did he?"

Barbie and the Freudian slip – Part Deux

While sitting around wrapping Christmas gifts this evening Barbie and I had the old Christmas classic by Rankin and Bass *Santa Claus Is Coming to Town*. As we were going through the gifts she held up a drinking glass emblazoned with pictures of Justin Bieber. Just to be clear she bought this cup for her 6-year-old cousin.

"I can't wait to give this to my little cousin", Barbie exclaimed. "She'll be so excited to be drinking a cup of Beaver...f**k, I mean Bieber."

After about ten seconds of letting it sink in, mixed with my laughter, Barbie muttered "Why does this always happen to me?"

I can only assume it happens for the amusement of us all.

Barbie's Original Freudian Slip

As promised here is the original story of Barbie and her Freudian slip of calling the Reese's Pieces candy Reese's Penis (thanks to a friend who was there for the story):

Barbie, Philip (my son who was about 13) and I went to Vaughan Mills for a day of shopping.

One of our stops was the Rocky Mountain Chocolate store.

At the back of the store are display cases with all of their feature apples. We went through a few of them--Basic Candy Apples, Oreo Cookie Apple.....

Barbie points to the glass and quite loudly says "look they even have Reese Penis".

5-4-3-2-1...here comes the look of horror as she plays back in her head what she had just said. The guy to the right of us is shocked, Philip walked away red-faced and I burst into laughter.

Barbie's face turns red and she asks if she really said what she thought she said....I was laughing so hard all I could do was nod.

At that point we left the store, buying nothing.

First Day of Christmas Break

As a closing out of 2011 I am going to tell the story of poor Barbie's first day of her Christmas vacation this year.

On Monday, last week, Barbie started her annual two-week sabbatical from her job. Barbie's little dog has recently been diagnosed with a partial ACL tear in her rear leg and to try to minimize the stress to the injury Barbie decided to carry her dog down the steps. As she was making her way down the stairs Barbie pulled a Barbie. She slipped and went down the last couple of steps bruising her forearm on the banister railing and on the steps she bruised her bum. The dog was fine however.

After kicking the day off to such a bang, Barbie went out to her bank to do some transactions. Upon leaving the bank she noticed a big, black garbage bag in the middle of parking lot. After reversing, and now having the bag in a blind spot, Barbie got ready to head home. Having cleared the bag, or so she thought, Barbie placed the car in drive and proceeded to leave the parking lot. However, she didn't clear the bag at all. Barbie's front wheels hit the garbage bag, and luckily for her, all that was in it was Styrofoam chip used for packing boxes. With the explosion of the chips Barbie's car was now covered in a protective layer of foam chips.

That night, while at figure skating, Barbie wiped out doing a jump and during the rotation landed completely wrong. Upon landing she bruised up her leg quite nicely, or quite sorely if you take her perspective, and thus proving that bad things do happen in sets of three.

Hydrasense Bukkake

Today while I was at work Barbie was at home convalescing from her battle with a bad cold and sinus infection that has been troubling her for about a week now. As I was working away I got an email from Barbie which caused me to laugh so hard I almost spit my drink out all over my keyboard...which would have been the second thing to be sprayed, but that's jumping the gun. Here is the email as it came to me:

While trying to put the Hydrasense nose spray in my nostril to clear my sinuses out, I pulled my face back too soon and shot it all over my face. I have a mint/eucalyptus spray in my eye.

When I finally got to speak to her and ask about it she said, "Have you ever used one of those things before?"

"Yes", I told her.

"I didn't know they were so powerful. I mean it was *whoosh!* And then it was all over my face."

Instantly I started laughing again and Barbie turned away...and I think she might have muttered a certain 7 letter word starting with an "A" in my direction too.

Barbie and the City of Yabba Dabba Doo

Sitting around the other day and Barbie mentions to me that her friend is going to Ethiopia for some charity work.

"Where in Ethiopia?" I asked.

"Adidas or something like that", she replied.

"You mean Addis Ababa?"

"Yeah that's it." Oh, if only that was it.

Fast forward 3 days later to dinner with Barbie and her brother over at the local Boston Pizza. During the dinner we were talking about the people we know and the latest news about them. Barbie mentions how the daughter of one of our train friends is contemplating going to spend a year in the Middle East nursing.

"She's looking at going to Qatar", I mention. I then proceed to mention how it's one of the more liberal nations in the Middle East. Beaches, women allowed to vote etc...

"Yeah it's one of the nicer sections, like Abu Dhabi", I concluded.

"Oh that's where my friend is going" Barbie chimes in.

"No, she isn't", I quickly corrected. "Abu Dhabi is in the Middle East. Your friend is going to Ethiopia - Addis Ababa."

"Right. Well I knew it was something that sounded like Yabba Dabba"

Barbie and Yabba Dabba Doo – Part Two

So on Monday night, not long after posting *Yabba Dabba Do*, Barbie and I were talking about the latest story.

"So I see you posted the Adababa story", she said to me.

"You mean Addis Ababa?" I asked.

"Well I knew it sounded like Abba so I was kinda right", Barbie said.

At this moment Barbie started humming and singing, at least the words she knew. This, in itself, was not as disturbing as you might think. What was being sung was the shock.

"Do, do, do, Heart of Glass" came out of Barbie's mouth.

"Are you singing..."

"Yeah Abba", she said cutting me off.

"Um, no. That's Blondie."

"Oh! Ok well then", to which she starts redoing Canadian Idol, "Call me, on the line, call me, call me any time."

"Uh, Blondie again", I told her.

"Oh, for the love of god. What the heck does Abba sing then?"

"Waterloo", I said to no response.

"Dancing Queen", I mentioned and no response.

"Take a chance on me", again to a blank stare.

"I don't know those ones. Maybe I don't know an Abba song after all. Can you sing one?"

So I proceeded to hum *Dancing Queen* and after about 20 seconds worth Barbie goes "Oh, I know that one"

And then she proceeded to carry on singing *Heart of Glass.*

Barbie Meet Cain

Last night after coming home from dinner with some friends I was telling Barbie about my discussion with the local door-to-door Religitarians on Saturday when I was out in the garage. So I was telling her about the picture they showed me and mention how that could be our street, with the fields, rivers, sunny skies and people all smiling while singing and dancing. I also mentioned at this point that I couldn't believe that picture would be my street because there are no houses and after years of hearing polka during Oktoberfest there was no way anyone would be having that much fun listening to accordion music. The Religitarian then went on to read a few verses from Psalms and told me that God would make this happen. "Man wasn't capable of ending wars. It would need to be God that did it."

At this point I mentioned how I wanted to tell the man God had promised to stay out man's affairs (Genesis 8:20-22) after he flooded the Earth and had made Noah save the animals two by two but figured I'd best keep my mouth shut so that the guy could finish his spiel, I could wish him well and see him off. So he carried on with his scripture lesson and then offered to leave some pamphlets and a book. I told Barbie "I told him 'No Thanks. I have two Bibles in the house that get read'."

Barbie then looks at me and goes "No we don't". I reminded her that I owned two Bibles and I had read them. "Oh right", Barbie said. "Yeah I have a kid's one somewhere I've never read. Maybe we should see if they have a children's Bible for the e-reader. Then I can learn all about that Horatio guy."

I admit that I have read the Bible but I don't have it memorized, although I do remember the majority of the stories. Horatio, however, was not one I remembered. "Horatio? Who the heck is Horatio", I asked.

"You know that guy. The one who killed his brother."

"You mean Cain? Like in Cain and Abel?"

About 10 seconds of uncomfortable silence passed when Barbie then slowly added "Uh, yeah. I meant Cain...you know...Horatio Cain"

"That's the clown in CSI: Miami" I blurt out.

"Well he has Cain in his name", Barbie retorted.

"Yeah, but I'm not sure it's spelt the same way. And he definitely wasn't called Horatio."

"Well he could have been", Barbie debated.

"Oh yeah, I can just imagine. Cain kills Abel and then next thing you know this ginger twit shows up going 'What I think we have here is murder' and flips up his bloody sunglasses", I responded.

Barbie just looked at me and went "It could have happened like that. After all, you weren't there so you don't know!"

I am going to look for that children's Bible in e-reader version now.

Barbie's Biblical Blunders

Well folks we came home and we started talking about the latest post (Barbie Meets Cain). I mentioned how there was a free e-book on the Kobo site that was a children's Bible (for the record the kid's Bibles are written in today's English unlike the actual Bible) and Barbie went and got the actual children's Bible she had on her bookshelf.

As she was flipping through the book she started asking me where she would find certain stories like Cain and Abel and Noah's flood. While we were flipping through Barbie came across a story called "On the Borders of Canaan". This is where it got good.

"Hey look. The borders of Canaan (but she pronounced it like K'naan the rapper)."

"Um, that's Canaan not Kay-non."

At this moment she started singing "Hey Ya". I looked at her and before I even said anything Barbie went "This isn't K'naan is it?"

"Nope, Outkast"

"Oh well", and she went back to singing Outkast.

Barbie's Butter Tart Delirium

Wow, on March 9th 2011 when I started documenting the adventures of Barbie I never thought I'd get to this point. The whole blog adventures came about when friends of ours, while listening to Barbie tell a story of her misadventures, laughed and said we should be documenting these stories. Honestly I figured this would only be read by a few close friends and never figured that in 11 months I would have 50 stories, over 1250 views and stories emailed to me asking if they were blog worthy for guest appearances. So ladies and gentlemen here is Barbie post number 50!

On New Year's Eve Barbie and I were going to drive up to visit her cousin for another raucous night of partying to ring in the New Year which we almost didn't see last year. So we scrambled around packing up our clothes, sleeping gear, dog and alcohol (which is mandatory for New Year's Eve partying). Once everything was packed, we loaded up the car and prepared for the hour-long drive to the 'Party Mansion'.

We got less than a minute away when the familiar chimes of uncertainty rang out in the car.

"Did I lock the house up?" Barbie asked.

"I dunno. But I guess we're turning around to check"

And turn around we did. As we pulled up to the house, after clocking a whopping 2 minutes and 10 seconds of road tripping, I mentioned to Barbie, "Don't forget to make sure you unplugged your straightening iron because I really don't want to turn around in another 3 minutes". I got the nice little sideways glance that is unmistakable in its meaning of "Shut up arsehole".

Twenty seconds later Barbie came back to the car, having checked and found that she had locked the door, and we were off again. As we backed out of the driveway I would be lying if I said I wasn't praying that we'd actually get out of the neighbourhood this time. Let me tell you that you really need to be careful what you ask for. We managed to make it out of the driveway and out of the neighbourhood. In fact we made it an entire 4km before Barbie pulled the car over onto the shoulder of the road.

"What is it now?" I asked.

"Um, I don't know if I packed my glasses or contacts."

"What do you mean you don't know?"

"Well I changed make up bags and now I'm not sure"

"You changed make up bags?"

"Yeah, I was getting tired of the other one so I switched"

"And now you don't know if you have your glasses or contacts, which were always in the other one"

"Um, yeah", Barbie said.

"So you forgot if you locked the door, forgot if you packed your glasses and what else did you manage to forget?" I queried.

"Look, I ate that butter tart and now I'm all confused."

Research Assistant Ken and the Solid Pipe

I was going to tell this story yesterday but since it was the 50th post I had to tell a Barbie related story, and since I've still got a few backlogged that I haven't written I figured it was a good time to spill one out. However, this story is about a co-worker of mine who is rather fond of the blog and laughs a lot at them when he hears them. And now, due to a momentary lapse of synapse connection, he is going to be immortalized as a guest post.

My place of work is one of the premier research hospitals in North America, and the top one in Canada. The tasks I have are to build prototypes of various devices, designed to assist patients and medical staff, which are tested and eventually put to market. One of these projects that we were building involved a metal frame bent into shape with various diameter pipes. One of the pipes wasn't holding the form it was designed to hold so we figured we'd bend some new pipe with a thicker wall and better stability.

As we were trying to manually bend the pipe without crimping it, because our pipe bender is out of commission at the moment, my co-worker came out with a suggestion of such magnitude and brilliance that I heard angels sing from the heavens...or maybe just the extreme loudness of my laughter.

"Hey", R.A. Ken says, "instead of using these pipes here wouldn't the project be much stronger if we use a solid pipe?"

"If we use a what?" I asked incredulously.

"A solid pipe."

"A solid pipe?" I asked again.

"Yeah a solid pipe. That would make it way stronger and spring back wouldn't it?" Ken asked.

"A solid effin' pipe?"

"Yeah a solid...pipe..." Ken repeated rather slowly as you could see the lights start to brighten inside his brain. "Dammit, you know what I meant. And you're going to blog this aren't you?"

"Oh yeah you know I will", I said. "A solid pipe hahahaha."

I walked back to office laughing my head off and really wondering whether a university degree is actually a good thing.

Haley Joel Osment sees Dead People and I see Barbies

OK, we are all familiar with the movie *Sixth Sense*. Even if you've never seen the movie you definitely know the scene where a young Haley Joel Osment tells Bruce Willis that he sees dead people. That line has been parodied in various Hollywood spoofs and even internet de-motivational posters (my favourite being the one that says "I see stupid people").

Well, not a lot unlike Haley Joel, I too see people...mine are living though. More importantly I see Barbie-esque style fails all around me. I'm starting to think that the creation of this blog has fine-tuned my inner senses to such actions and this week has been good. We'll start with the Barbies-in-training, and two Kens-in-training, before going on to our actual Barbie.

Yesterday, while going to get lunch at the Ontario Power Generation building, I witnessed three instances of Barbie-isms within 3 minutes. While making my way to the Tim Horton's for a sandwich and tea I witnessed a lady walk up to the revolving door and push with all her might. Not once. Not twice. But three different times this poor woman shoved with all her might and the door wouldn't budge. At this moment, with a great moment of intellectual clarity, the woman turned around 180 degrees and after making a quick check that she didn't know anyone, pushed on the opposite glass pane. You know, the one with the handle attached - unlike the one she was previously shoving. Miraculously the door rotated and this lady was freed.

Right after this little moment I went into Tim Horton's and witnessed more follies. As I was standing in line making my order I overheard the young lady working announce the order she brought to the counter. "Boston Cream doughnut and a medium double-double", announced the Tim's employee. I noticed a guy standing beside, who looked like a local university student, pull out a receipt from his pocket. Read this receipt over with great intensity. Look up at the counter, back at the receipt and then back at the counter. Having fully deduced that this massive ordering of food was indeed his to enjoy he proceeded to put away the receipt and grab the food and drink.

A mere 30 seconds later, as I finished making my order, the same employee came up and announced another order. "Bagel with cream cheese and a medium regular", she announced. Standing beside me was another university looking guy with a skateboard. I had a moment of Deja vu then as this guy also took out his receipt, read through it with the same scrutiny as the previous student and then took his food as well. When my order came up I took it, without scanning my receipt, turned around and noticed that both of these young guys happened to be sitting at the same table. I have to admit I was snickering as I was leaving to go back to work.

And now for the main event...

Today riding home from the train the 'real' Barbie of this blog was sitting there on the phone with a call from work. During this conversation Barbie started rifling through her purse aimlessly. Suddenly the purse shuffling became more intense. Barbie was holding her Blackberry case in her hand and looking around for her phone. A look of panic came on her face as she mouthed the words "Where's my Blackberry?" I looked at her sort of weirdly and before I could mutter anything at all our dear Barbie had it click that she was holding her Blackberry in one hand, since she was talking on it, and the case in the other.

Yes folks I see Barbies...they are everywhere.

Barbie and the X-Men

Last night while sifting through Netflix looking for something watch we stumbled across a British show called *Eleventh Hour* starring Patrick Stewart.

"Oh, it's that Magnesium dude", Barbie exclaimed.

"Magnesium?!?" I said confused.

"Yeah from X-Men"

"Um, that would be Magneto", I answered and before I could continue my sentence...

"Oh right", said Barbie.

"And that's not Magneto either. It's Charles Xavier."

"Whatever, close enough"

"Odd, most people know him as Jean-Luc Picard from Star Trek"

"You're such a nerd", was Barbie's answer and last words in this conversation - because she's right.

It's called a wreathe?

We were riding on one of the late commuter trains home just before Christmas and we overheard a conversation between four other riders.

"Hey, do you guys know where I could buy a reef?" asked a male rider who was about 40ish and will be Rider #1 from here out.

Rider #2, who was a female about 50ish, answered him "Um, in almost any store. Home Depot, Canadian Tire, Walmart. Just pick one"

"Really? Home Depot?" asked Rider #1.

"Yeah you can get them in Home Depot", replied Rider #3 - another male in his 40's.

"Wow. I was in Home Depot and they told me they didn't sell them. I walked up to one of the kids and asked him where they keep the reefs", mentioned Rider #1.

"Wait a minute", chipped in Rider #4 (another female but in her 40's), "did you say reef or wreathe?"

"Reef. Why?" asked Rider #1

A few chuckles started among Rider #1's fellow riders at this point.

"It's a wreathe. A reef is marijuana", Rider #4 informs Rider #1.

"What? Really? Man no wonder the kids wouldn't show me. I'm in asking for marijuana instead of a Christmas decoration?" states Rider #1. "Oh geez, I can't go back to that Home Depot anymore. Those kids will think I'm a drug officer and man, this explains why those kids were snickering too"

We were busting a gut all the way home from the train station laughing at how someone in their 40's didn't know the difference between a reef and wreathe however.

Barbie and the Whore of Akron

On the weekend Barbie and I were in the local Chapters bookstore shopping around for books. One of the books Barbie stumbled across was one called *The Whore of Akron.*

"Oh that will be about LeBron James", I mention to Barbie as I see her opening the cover.

After a few seconds of perusing the write up inside the book's jacket she looks at me and says "This is about LeBron James"

"Um, yeah that's what I told you"

"No you said Ron Jeremy!"

"Let's see - LeBron is from Akron and bolted from Cleveland's basketball team to Miami because they promised a dynasty and NBA championship and that's a silhouette of LeBron on the cover. I don't even know where Ron Jeremy is from so I say again that I said LeBron James"

Looking somewhat dumbfounded Barbie says "Why did I hear Ron Jeremy?"

Apparently our friend Barbie has been surfing the dirty sections on the internet.

Barbie and the X-Men 2

Last night we were watching the movie *Goon* with Seann William Scott (better known as Stiffler from American Pie). While watching the movie there is a scene when Stiffler's character, Doug Glatt, is talking to the movie's antagonist Ross Rhea, played by Liev Schreiber.

"I recognize the other guy. Who is it?" Barbie asks me.

"That's Liev Schreiber."

"Oh yeah, Wolfgang's brother", Barbie quips in.

"Wolfgang? Oh for the love of God, you mean Wolverine", I reply.

Instant laughter from Barbie as she realizes her flub and goes "Whatever, it's his brother right. Tigerman or something"

"Sabre-tooth, and yes they were brothers"

"Knew it"

And we went back to watching the movie, and I'm sure aliens have lobotomized Barbie.

Engineering Barbie and the Screwdriver

It's been a while since Engineering Barbie made an appearance but she's in fine form today. While helping the Industrial Designer build a test wall at my work good old Engineering Barbie struck a gem today.

"Hey Steve, I hope this is the right size screwdriver", states E.B.

Steve looks at the tool for a second and looks up and says "This is a wrench. I don't need this, I need a screwdriver."

Apparently I need to revisit the Tool Classification Chart with Engineering Barbie.

A Barbie Moment Leads To a Hot Tub Exposure...Almost

One day last week a co-worker of dear Barbie, and someone who has been a guest in the blog, was working last week from home. During this time she decided to go and take a break in her hot tub. Now, being the middle of the day when everyone else is working and living in the middle of nowhere, our dear Barbie-in-Training decided to hot tub in her birthday suit.

So as she is hot tubbing away without a lick of clothing on our Barbie-in-Training hears a noise. Very quickly she assesses this to be the oil truck. And even quicker she figures 'Oh lord, the oil-man is here to fill our oil-tanks'.

Scrambling she gets out of the hot tub in her skin suit and in doing so falls down getting out of the hot tub. Once on the ground she began to wrestle with her bathrobe so that she can cover up. In doing so she managed to get the robe half way on and realized that one of the tie up straps was caught in the crack of her bum. After fighting with it for a while she managed to get it unstuck and tied her robe up just as the oil-man opened the gate to the backyard.

So in walks the oil-man and our Barbie-in-Training is still in a squatting position. With a quick mind instead of trying to explain why she was squatted down our poor friend pretended to start cleaning the walls of the hot tub so that the oil-man wouldn't ask what she was doing.

Colour Blind and Spatially Challenged

Ok folks this is a two for one deal today since I've been rather neglectful in posting.

So on Sunday we were driving to Guelph and Barbie was eating an apple in the car. She finished the apple and decided she would toss it into the field since were on a country road, and let's remember before the littering comments start that it is biodegradable. So she rolls the window down and decides to toss it with her left hand. Now please envision this as Barbie was sitting in the passenger side of the car, is right-handed and could have easily put her arm out the window and just let go. That would be the easy way. Barbie decided to go the hard way. She took the apple in her left hand and swung it across her body to throw the apple out the window. However, as she released the apple it ricocheted off the inside door frame and rebounded into gear shift casing and then fell to the floor.

"I thought you played baseball?" I asked.
"I did play baseball" she says defensively while tossing the apple out this time. "That was my wrong hand"
"You were all off 6 inches from the window and missed? And why wouldn't you just use your right hand?"
"Whatever, it's out the window now."

I continued to drive on still laughing my head off, and to be honest Barbie was giggling herself at the fiasco that occurred. The irony in this is Barbie used to be a pitcher for the town she lived in and school she went to.

Barbie's Day Out

On Wednesday last week Barbie had some running around to do. Her first stop was for a medical appointment she had when she noticed an Italian eatery in the same strip mall. Since she had some time available Barbie decided to give the diner a try. She went in for lunch. Barbie ordered herself a salad and the clerk asked her what she would like on it.

"I'd like to have some onions, tomatoes, croutons, cheese, computers..."

At that point Barbie realized that she had made quite the faux pas on her order and started laughing. "Oh my god. I want cucumbers not computers. That would be weird"

Barbie got her salad, without further incident, and proceeded about her day. Everything else flowed easily until she went to Walmart to do some shopping. While in Walmart Barbie felt the call of nature come about and went to the bathroom. As she was sitting in the stall the person in the stall next to her flushed the toilet. It seems, on top of having cheap merchandise, Walmart also skimped out on their plumbing costs. Immediately after that toilet was flushed there was a bit of a mild explosion in Barbie's stall. Not the type of explosion one would normally associate with going to the bathroom but rather the water in the toilet bowl that Barbie was sitting on shot up like a mini-Old Faithful and soaked Barbie butt. Luckily for Barbie she hadn't actually done anything so all she got was a little wet.

Chef Boy-ar-Barbie

One night Barbie and her brother were hanging out and Barbie offered to cook dinner. She had recently come into possession of a recipe for macaroni and cheese from a friend. Now, for those unaware, Barbie isn't exactly what you would call kitchen savvy. Utilizing her Blackberry email, Barbie was going to cook up a storm. Going step by step she went through the recipe and made a really good batch of macaroni and cheese for herself and her brother.

Feeling quite content with her accomplishment she took out the bowls to serve her this successful concoction she cooked up. She scooped the mac-n-cheese into the bowls and proceeded to carry them into the dining area. As she was putting the bowls down the unforeseeable happened. Do you think she managed to keep the food in the bowls and not dump it on the floor? Well, surprisingly, she did. Do you think she whacked the table, as in the past, and spilt some of the drinks that were on the table? That didn't happen either. No, as our dear friend Barbie was putting the bowls on the table the Blackberry, which she was using to read the recipe, fell out from under her armpit and dropped into one of the bowls.

So there they both stood staring at the bowls with one having a Blackberry stuck in the mac-n-cheese and standing straight up. Being a work issued Blackberry poor Barbie had a bit of a meltdown. Her brother, being somewhat technically adept, told her to go grab some rubbing alcohol and Q-tips. He proceeded to work his magic and get the cheese out of the keys of the Blackberry thus bringing it to a perfect working state.

Barbie – Master of the Smoothie

The other day for lunch, Barbie decided that she was going to go the healthy route and make herself a smoothie to quell her appetite. Being somewhat of a pro at these things (since she tends to make them at least once a week, it seems), Barbie went and grabbed all her ingredients and utensils required. Out came the Magic Bullet, the frozen yoghurt and the frozen berries and fruits.

Barbie loaded the fruits and berries into the Magic Bullet, added some yoghurt and prepped the Bullet to be the creator of smoothies. However, before starting on this divine creation for her lunch, Barbie began to clean up...sort of.

Barbie proceeded to zip up the bag of frozen berries and took them to the freezer. As she put the bag into the freezer a minor continental shift occurred with the Earth's tectonic plates - or so Barbie would like me to believe. The bag, by some form of miracle, shifted when being placed in the freezer setting off a chain reaction. Following the shift Barbie witnessed the frozen yoghurt being knocked out of the freezer as if being part of some weird nutritious game of King of the Hill. This was not the end of the chain reaction, unfortunately. Next came the bag of fruit and I do mean the same bag that started this reaction. The bag managed tipped over and emptied all over the kitchen floor.

Barbie stood there and stared at the menagerie of fruit scattered over the kitchen floor. It took a minute, possibly two, of staring dumb-founded at what had just occurred in front of her very eyes. Once reality kicked back in and Barbie accepted what happened, she decided, "I better clean this up".

So Barbie went to get her broom and dustpan with the hopes of cleaning up. Well, even the best laid plans suffer a hiccup sometimes, and in this case, that hiccup was that the fruit had begun thawing. As Barbie was sweeping up her spill, she began to notice that the raspberries, blueberries and mangos were leaving colourful streaking across the kitchen floor.

Barbie opened up the freezer door again and noticed some unsuccessful escapees were scattered amongst the shelving of the freezer. Picking out the stray bits from the shelving Barbie managed to get her freezer cleaned up and resettled the formation of the products inside. However, this was not the end of the cleaning. Poor Barbie had to wash the broom and dustpan out to remove the residue left by the varying fruits so she took them outside and sprayed them down with a hose. Then came the kitchen floor cleanup, which at this point was looking almost like a scene from Dexter or CSI. After washing the floor, Barbie then noticed that pieces of raspberry had made their way on the carpet in the living room and she then proceeded to scrub the carpet as well to prevent staining.

Finally, after all was said and done, Barbie was able to make her smoothie although I'm sure it tasted a little bitter after the experience.

Barbie Learns About Necking

This story was relayed to me about an incident before Barbie and I met. I've had a few requests for this story and when I asked about it, I have to admit I laughed very hard over this.

Barbie was over at her aunt and uncle's house for a family gathering when her father and step-mom disappeared from the party. Once they were gone for a little while, her uncle piped up, in more humorous manner, "I bet they went out necking". Of course, everyone laughed, except for Barbie, her brother and her two step-sisters who sort of giggled while controlling their inner disgust. Let's be honest - no child wants to think of their parent getting any action beyond a handshake or hug.

A few hours later on the ride home, Barbie mentioned the comment to her friend. "What was that? Uncle Peter made that comment about my dad and step-mom necking. I mean, like, ewww.... And who would do that, anyway? What possible pleasure can two people get from rubbing their necks together? Gross." Barbie truly believed that necking was the act of rubbing necks together, similar to the childhood game where you pass an orange between two people.

Our dear friend Barbie is lucky to be alive today because the blank look on the face of her travelling companion almost led to a car crash...probably because Barbie was 25 years old and still didn't get the concept of necking.

Engineering Barbie Also Needs Facial Recognition Programming

Today at lunch I was sitting with two co-workers, one of which was Engineering Barbie and the other was Research Assistant Ken. While we were eating lunch the following conversation came about:

"Do you know what song is stuck in my head? That 'Funky Mother' song". This resulted in somewhat confused looks so Engineering Barbie elaborated.

"You know the one", and she starts to hum a tune and then lowly sing the following, "...right about now, that funky mother, right about now"

At this point R.A. Ken and I started howling. "That's Fatboy Slim", replied R.A. Ken in between spurts of laughter. I added to the answer with the proper lyrics by saying, "You mean 'Right about now, the funk soul brother' don't you?"

Immediately I opened up YouTube and found a video for the song. "Yeah that's the song. Now imagine that being stuck in your head for the entire team meeting", asked Engineering Barbie.

At this point I decided to try to stick another song in her head and said, "Well you could have this one instead."
I clicked on the link for *Snap!* singing "I've Got the Power".

Once this video started and the lead rapper, Turbo B, appeared poor Engineering Barbie fell into the 'Barbie-Zone' - which is kind of like the Twilight Zone but you see acts of goofiness instead of the weird.

"Oh my god, that's the guy from Hot Tub something or other."

At this moment there was a combined jaw drop as we turned to look at her. R.A. Ken started killing himself laughing. I, on the other hand, looked at Engineering Barbie and said "Um, no. Completely different dudes". Then to make matters a little more humorous, well at least for myself, I added "Not all black folks look-alike."

Showing just how certain she was, Engineering Barbie started defending her case. "No, look they have the same eyes"

"What? Dark brown? The majority of black people have eyes like that."

A little frustrated now she pointed out Exhibit B, "Look they have the same nose"

"Yeah, most black people have that nose style. In fact they even joke about it and call it a black nose."

Engineering Barbie asked me to open a picture of Craig Robinson, and for the record she called him 'the dude from the hot tub thingie movie', so she could prove her case. So I went to IMDB.com and found a picture of him.   So on one screen I had the music video and on the other screen I had a picture of Craig from the movie and it began.

"Look the nose is the same", Engineering Barbie exclaimed.

"You mean except for the mole on the left side of the one guy's nose right?" I asked not so innocently.

"Oh, um, yeah. Ok maybe they aren't the same...or maybe he had it removed!"

"They aren't the same. Not all black people look-alike. And these two dudes are certainly different, much like the other two you tend to confuse", I added.

"Who else did she confuse?" asked R.A. Ken.

"Hulk Hogan and Mr. T, as they are apparently similar looking too."

"WHAT?!?!?!?" exclaimed R.A. Ken right before he turned beet red from laughing so hard.

Engineering Barbie chirped her two cents in with, "Well they are both really big muscular guys."

"Yeah except Mr. T is like 5'4" and black while Hogan, although tanned, is 6'7" and white", I mentioned.

"Whatever, the one looks like he should be called Mr. T anyways. I'm going back to work"

And with that dear Engineering Barbie stomped off to her work station.

Barbie Gets Tongue Tied

On Saturday there was a tragic incident in Toronto at the Eaton Centre shopping mall downtown. Sadly, a complete idiot decided to fire a gun off in a crowded mall in an act of revenge on some people and in the process hurt many others.

One of those injured was a pregnant lady who was trampled in the rush of people who were running out of fear since the shooter decided, instead of shooting the people he was having issues with, shot his first bullet into the air and thus created a human version of the chaos theory with everyone running like frightened gazelles. On a positive note, both the mother and newly born child are doing well.

As we were discussing the story the topic of the pregnant lady came up. Barbie, with a little bit of disgust in her tone of voice, spoke of her displeasure of the crowd's behaviour. "I can't believe they trampeded a pregnant woman."

"Oh, no kidding", I said.

At this moment I clued in that something wasn't quite right. With my head cocked at a slight angle, much like a confused dog, I asked the question "Wait, what did you call it? Trampeded?!?"

With a little less certainty Barbie answered. "Well, I meant Stampled."

I started snickering at this moment having been witness to another verbal screw up.

With some frustration Barbie groaned, "Argh! Why can't I say the words I want!!!"

I have to admit she may have gotten it right after that sentence but I couldn't hear a word poor Barbie was saying. I was laughing too hard for her to be heard for about the next 20 minutes to be honest.

Barbie's Tea, Toast and the Spill of Doom

Good Afternoon readers. Today we have a special guest blogger contributing to the Barbie Fails saga. Kyle is a co-worker of Barbie's and he was eye-witness to a special display typical of our poor Barbie this morning. This is the recap he sent to me when I heard there was a bit of misadventure:

"I saw Barbie walking into the self-serve Tim's and having known her for a few years, was optimistically expecting a decent show of some sort. Barbie sees me, says "Hey! How are you?" and I actually think this is what set the events in motion since now there was the pressure of having someone she knows behind her in the line.

Barbie selects her tea from the choices (she was shielding this part with her body, not sure if she put something extra in her cup or not). After blocking both the tea and coffee sections for a couple of minutes while she struggled with selecting milk size and amount, she makes her way off to the side to remove the tea bag and add the lid. I've bought Barbie tea before, I know she keeps the bag in for a bit so she can steep the tea, so I was surprised to see her fiddling with the tea bag, like she was going to take it out. Her next move is where it got interesting. In a move similar to a cowboy flicking a whip, she managed to yank/snap her tea bag out of her cup, while spilling roughly half her tea back onto the counter and floor, and throws the bag onto the floor (she's standing beside the garbage hole, designed for tea bags, stir sticks etc.).

Barbie has everyone in lines attention now, mainly because she is blocking us all, and is clearly flustered. After walking around in a circle twice she decides she should clean up her mess, with the one napkin she has in her hand. I take this opportunity to ask "Do you work from home a lot Barbie? Clearly you aren't used to being in a public setting." People are politely trying to walk around Barbie and her mess, while she uses her foot and napkin to push the tea on the floor around, increasing the size of the spill. She manages to track down more napkins, tidies up the tea on the counter and floor and lines up to pay. I can see her searching pockets and trying to juggle her half a cup of tea (she didn't refill the spilled amount) and toast and she turns to me and says "Crap Kyle, I think I lost my money, I may need you to pay for me". After a show like that, I truly felt like I owed Barbie something and would have been more than happy to pay her for the show (think of contributing to a buskers act by giving them a toonie or some change). She locates her money and manages to pay for her tea and toast without any further incidents. At this point I haven't heard if there was anything else exciting about the tea and toast...."

Barbie Gets a Lesson in Multi-Culturism

Two weeks ago Barbie was watching "America's Got Talent" when a young man named Edon took the stage to perform. When he took the stage he sat down to a piano and began to play the song "Titanium". As this Edon was singing Barbie mentioned out loud

"He's doing a pretty good version of Adele here". This was sort of a fail in two regards. First, the song wasn't performed by Adele and, more importantly, second that I had no idea that Barbie was wrong. Unfortunately, when it comes to popular music I haven't had my finger on the pulse since about 1994.

Being as I was on my computer, probably watching wrestling of some sort, I wasn't fully paying attention. Due to this I muttered "What guy?"

"The Jewish kid on the piano", Barbie replied.

"How do you know he's Jewish?" I asked, since I hadn't really looked up from the computer I hadn't even seen the kid on the television yet.

"Uh, he's got one of those ramekins on his head."

At this moment I looked up. However, I looked up more out utter confusion than out of curiosity. "A ramekin?!?!?"

"Yeah those things on their head", Barbie answered.

"They are called 'yah-mu-kaus' ", I told her. "And they spell it y-a-r-m-u-l-k-e-s."

"Oh, so that's what a 'yar-mulk-ahs' is. I always wondered what that was whenever I saw that word at work and in books"

I went back to my computer, zoned out with whatever I was watching and awaited the Rod Serling voice over telling me that I had entered "The Barbie Zone".

OMG, Where is My Purse?

Yesterday was a rather trying day for Barbie at work for many reasons but the Barbie Fails moment came at the end of the day.

As the day came to a close Barbie went to get her purse as she was packing up to leave for the day. Since the workstations have drawers for you to put your belongings in, desks are not permanent but rather signed out by employees so you may not have the same desk daily, Barbie had placed her purse inside the drawer that seemed to correspond with her desk. From here I give you the play-by-play in Barbie's own words:

When I realized my purse was trapped in the bottom drawer, I exclaimed "OMG, my purse is locked in the drawer and Karen's gone home for the night". Laury and I ran to the window of the 26th floor and saw that her car had already left the Roy Thompson Hall parking lot. I ran to find another lady with the hope of finding a spare key, but upon searching her collection, we noted it was missing. Laury called someone else to see if they had a key; also came up empty. At that point, we started to laugh uncontrollably and decided it was the funniest thing that had happened all day.

My purse spent the night, alone, locked in the bottom drawer.

And the offending co-workers version of events, after they had realized what happened:

Very sorry...I didn't even think you were using the drawers as I saw your backpack on the floor and thought that's all you had. I used that set of drawers as there is no key where I was at, it won't happen again, I'm so sorry.

The best part of all this was a somewhat flustered, yet in good spirits, Barbie getting into my car explaining what had happened and then realizing "I have no money, no I.D., no cell phone and no car keys. So it's a good thing you're the one driving".

For the record I'm always the one driving when it comes to going to Toronto for work ;)

My Mum + Barbie = Me Shaking My Head All Night

Last night my dad turned 63 and for his birthday Barbie and I arranged to take him to dinner. We arrived at my parents' house last night, around 5.30ish, to pick them up and head to the local pub. With it being a Friday, and being his birthday probably didn't hurt, my dad had started the festivities a little early with some rye and cokes.

So, after a couple of beers and my dad have 2 or 3 drinks himself, we set off to the local for some drinks and food. Barbie, who wasn't drinking, drove everyone over to the bar in my parents' Kia Rondo. When we got there my dad told Barbie to back into one of the spaces and Barbie told him "Oh no, I don't do reverse parking. I do forward parking". Now, anyone who has ever been in the car with Barbie when she tries to reverse in can attest that it is not a thing of beauty to watch but rather painful.

Succumbing to the pseudo peer pressure coming from my dad Barbie decided she'd back up into the parking spot, which luckily for all of us was actually 5 spots that were empty. So as we pull up to the spots Barbie stops directly perpendicular to the parking spaces, in essence forcing a 90 degree turn needed to back into the spot. "Well, I can see why you aren't good at reversing, you've completely cut off your angle", my dad chimes in.

"That's why I drive in", Barbie added. So she began to back up and turning the wheel. Attempt number one ended with Barbie being parked on the middle of the line between two spots. "Oh, that didn't work so well", Barbie states.

As she goes and starts to drive forward my dad adds in the comment "You see those two things there?"
He was pointing to the side mirrors when he asked. "If you look in them you can see the lines."
"I never really use them", Barbie admitted. My dad started laughing while I sat in the back shaking my head for the first time that night.

Attempt number two began with Barbie driving forward and attempting to line herself up with the cars in front of her as she figured she could just drive straight back if she was aligned. Smart idea and to be honest I can't fault that logic, however, the best laid plans as the saying goes. Barbie felt comfortable and competent in her vehicular placement and then proceeded to place the car in reverse. So far so good but that only lasted about 3 seconds.

As the car started moving backwards Barbie began turning the wheel. Unfortunately for Barbie she didn't need to move the wheel all that much and she would have been in the space, although probably not exactly in the middle. That didn't happen though. Barbie spun the wheel too much and wound up right back where she started - on top of the yellow line straddling two spaces. Shaking my head yet again I mentioned that I would get out and go get our table. My dad said "Right, let me show how this is done".

Barbie, my mum and myself were standing outside the car while my dad got into the driver's seat, keep in mind he had a few drinks to boot, and pulled the car forward, then backward and in one stab managed to get the car straight smack in the middle of the parking spot. Getting out of the vehicle my dad said "Let's go eat", and I have to admit I was snickering a little.

As we were sitting around the table with the first round of beverages were on table, Guinness for the men, vodka and water for my mum and cranberry and soda for Barbie. It was decided that we'd just feast on a bunch of appetizers instead of ordering actual meals for the night. We then proceeded to decide which appetizers to feed on and the shake my head moment number three arrived. My mum while looking at the menu came across something referred to as Tattie Fritters Supreme, which is thinly sliced battered potatoes deep-fried with cheese and bacon topping them. Up seeing these my mum went "Oh, I think I'd like to try these Tittie Fratters". Barbie caught this faux pas and mentioned "I think you mean Tattie Fritters not Tittie Fratters" while starting to giggle.

I really don't think I can allow these two women out in public, with access to alcohol, anymore.

Sauble Barbie's Emancipation

Last week Barbie told me a story of her co-worker, who owns a cottage in Sauble Beach, who we shall refer to as Sauble Barbie.

It turns out that the first Saturday in August there is an Emancipation Party held in Owen Sound, Ontario. A follow-up party is held the next day in Sauble Beach. Sauble Barbie was asked to go to the party on the Sunday, which is hosted by a couple who live nearby. In Sauble Barbie's own words here's what happened:

I was invited to an emancipation party but had no idea what that meant. Apparently it is an annual celebration on the first Saturday of every August in Owen Sound and it is followed up by a celebration the next day (Sunday) in Sauble Beach. A mixed race couple hosts the party in Sauble every year. At the party on Sunday I thought I heard the reason for the celebration was because of the blacks' involvement in the railroad. So I thought they helped build the railroad. Even though I couldn't picture any railroad in Owen Sound. A week later I was retelling my story and when I came to the part about the railroad and Ray (Sauble Barbie's husband) stopped me and said "You're joking right". He then went on to explain it was the "underground railroad where black slaves were smuggled to freedom". So the party was to celebrate freedom. Can't say I was ever a history buff. But I did have a blast at the party.

I can honestly say I can only imagine something like this happening to the Barbie Gang.

Barbie Has a Chernobyl Style Meltdown

Yesterday was a very eventful day here in Barbie World. It started with the morning medicating of her dog Chelsea, who is a Shetland Collie. On Tuesday it was confirmed that Chelsea had a doggie version of an ACL tear in her right hind leg. So on Thursday Chelsea went into surgery for the repairs to be done which is actually called 'Tightrope CCL Surgery'. One of the three medications sent home was Rimadryl, which is a non-steroidal anti-inflammatory drug used as a pain-killer for dogs. The bigger problem with Rimadryl is the fact that it is somewhat toxic to cats and Barbie, of course, owns a cat.

So on Friday morning while feeding the dog her Rimadryl, which she was supposed to take a full pill and half of another pill, by mixing the medication with some Beneful wet-food for the dog. However, as anyone who has owned two pets, you can't feed one without the other. So Barbie proceeded to feed the cat some of his wet food. This is where the panic and eventual meltdown started.

So I came down the stairs to make some morning tea and there is Barbie in full panic and almost in tears. "I think I've killed the cat", where the words I was met with. Of course when I looked over her shoulder there is Dexter, the cat, sitting on his little table eating and as content as anything.

"Um, no you didn't. He's sitting right there as happy as Larry", I said to her.

"No, I've killed him."

"How in the heck did you kill the cat this time?" I asked. Note I said this time. We have gone down this path before, including one incident where she thought the cat had been licking at a spot in the floor that Barbie had cleaned with Javex.

"I fed Chelsea and gave her the Rimadryl", she blubbered out. "And..." I stated.

"And I used the same fork for both their meals and I think he might have got some medication too."

"What do you mean you think he got some? Isn't it a pill?"

"Yes but the half pill might have stuck to the fork and now I've killed the cat. I have to call the vet and get his stomach pumped."

"No we don't. The pill didn't stick to the fork. And the cat will be fine"

So this went on for a few more minutes with Barbie getting more and more upset to where the tears had started. About this time Barbie's brother arrived at the house and the whole conversation above started again. Only this time more agitated and stressed out on Barbie's end. Her brother would eventually ask how you know that's toxic to the cat and the answer came "I looked it up on the internet. And I poisoned him. And he's going to get seizures, and his kidneys will fail and..."

"Oh lord, you need to stay off the internet. In fact we should take the internet away from you"

At this point Barbie's mum had called and things just snowballed even more. When Barbie got on the phone the water works started again as she tried to tell her mum she had killed the cat. As we sat listening to Barbie tearfully mumble her story all we could hear on the other end was her mum going "What? Start again. I can't understand a word you've said".

So Barbie went through the story at least two more times before she was actually coherent enough to be understood. Once the story came out Barbie's brother and I could just hear this loud burst of laughter from the other end of the phone. Apparently Barbie's mum also found this as humorous as the rest of us...well except Barbie she wasn't humoured as all. When we finally got Barbie settled down she adamantly stated "If my cat dies all of you arseholes are chipping in to buy me a new one".

The rest of the day was uneventful until bed time when Barbie removed her contacts and then 30 seconds later tried to remove them again and scratched her eye resulting in her having to wear glasses for today. As a follow-up here are some of Barbie's internet research follies:

1. panicked that she poisoned the cat with Rimadryl
2. thought she had developed Parkinson's when her hands started shaking (it was a hyper-active thyroid)
3. thought she had developed lymphoma when she thought her lymph nodes had swollen (it was due to some close shaving in her grooming it turns out)
4. her dog's limp was originally a grass seed trapped in her paw and worked its way into her leg (another internet find)
5. the cat ate a small metal ring, used for making bracelets, and it was going to rip his intestines open
6. the dog started vomiting, after my mum gave her a sausage, and Barbie was convinced it was a twisted stomach and not just an intolerance to the sausage

So as you can see Barbie is a little bit of a hypochondriac and the internet is at times the worst enemy instead of being a tool of resource.

Potential Barbie Candidates and Opening Doors

Yesterday I was at the Atrium on Bay in downtown Toronto grabbing some lunch with a co-worker. As we were standing in line the first of many humorous events occurred. That being the gentleman who passed by us with his tray of food. This gentleman was wearing penny loafer style shoes with some of the tightest pants I've ever seen a man wear. To top that off they were capris. Adding to the attire of this fashion plate was a bright yellow wife-beater style shirt, with an unbuttoned short sleeve Hawaiian shirt over it. Lastly he had a big wide yellow head band, which looked like a scarf tied around his noggin, and the long dangling ends of this scarf/wrap hanging loose around his 80's style rocker hair. He looked like a genetic experiment made from some rock-n-roll version of "The Island of Doctor Moreau" using DNA from Boy George, Mark Knopfler (Dire Straits) and Platinum Blonde.

As we were sitting eating, after getting our food with little incident, I noticed a lady walk up to the doors that exit the food court to Bay Street. She proceeded to pull on the doors which failed to open. So she pulled a little harder but with each tug she would put a little forward momentum into the door to get that extra 'oomph' out. Of course with each moment going forward the door would open and then quickly close as she yanked it toward thinking that the doors that push really needed to be pulled. This exercise in futility occurred about 4 or 5 times before she surrendered to the door and decided it was locked. Moving on the next door down the line she proceeded to go through the exact same motions again. With each attempt she was getting more and more violent in her use of force in trying to pull this door open, and with each forward motion made you could see the door opening before being yanked closed by her own hand yet again. Deciding this door was also locked she moved down to the last door in that line.

In an almost Herculean feat of strength she began pulling the door. At one point I thought she might have had a moment of clarity when she realized the door pushed not pulled open but it turns out that it was just me overestimating her grasp on the mechanics of the door. She yanked and pulled with all the might she could muster in her little 100 pound frame and then let out a cry of frustration and kicked the door. Standing beside her was mall security, who had been talking to the mall custodian and missed the entire display it seems, and he leaned over and went "Excuse me ma'am, but the doors push". He then gave the doors a little shove forward and they opened. The poor woman, who was flustered and probably more than a little embarrassed, scurried out like a mouse on speed. I've never seen someone move so quick that wasn't in the Olympics.

Barbie Drops In

On Monday, while at work, Barbie had a bit of a gymnastics moment but not quite at the '10' level of a Mary Lou Retton or Nadia Comaneci. As Barbie was walking down one of the aisles at work, and past a full meeting room, she managed to get the tip of her shoe trapped into the cuff of her pants. Unable to stop the physical momentum that was driving her forward, Barbie would wind up going into a full somersault and finishing it in a cross-legged position while sitting on her butt inside the conference room.

Without missing a beat Barbie looked up at the stunned attendees as she said "Hi, how is everyone? I thought I'd drop in and check on you."

She would get up, brush herself off and walk out. The folks having the meeting were still somewhat dumbstruck as they witnessed the entire incident from the start since the meeting room's walls were made of glass and they could see everything that was happening in the office area.

Bolshevik Ken and the Metal Conundrum

For those unaware I work in a metal shop making parts for one of the research hospitals in Toronto and my usual story time subject is Barbie, who works at one of the bank head offices in Toronto as well. So this story actually involves me and not Barbie this time.

This morning I was writing up S.O.P's, which are *Standard Operation Procedures*, for the various machines I am responsible for because our Occupation Health and Safety department has decided that they require copies for their records. While typing these forms up one of the contractors here at work came into my shop. This gentleman is responsible for building a motion platform in one of the research labs and apparently some of their pieces didn't fit properly. So he comes into my shop looking for me to do some retrofit modifications to his parts and in his Russian accented voice says to me:

"My friend, I need these modified to this", and he pulls out a drawing that they have hand written some changes on. "I have 4 of these in total", he says.

So I look at the pieces, which are metallic but painted so I'm not sure whether it was cast iron or steel and better yet if steel what type and was it heat-treated.

"You can place them on that work bench", I say pointing to the nearest mill. "What kind of material is this?"

He stands there and looks at me for a little while and says "Oh, they are metal". And this he turns and leaves as I stand there thinking to myself that this is a flipping machine shop and everything here is metal.

I swear I must have some sort of magnetic draw to conversations and incidents like this.

Kens Shouldn't Exercise

I love that I have very interactive readers. The other day I was approached by a lady I work with about a brilliant "Barbie Fails" style screw up from a conference she was at. While at this conference my associate, who we shall call Julie (since no one gets their real name used), was working out in the fitness room of the hotel she was staying at.

In the middle of Julie's workout she heard a male voice burst out in what could be described as unexpected shock and awe...and not in a good manner. Quickly turning her head Julie managed to catch the tail end of a man being shot off the treadmill and another man sitting on his arse quickly apologizing. According to Julie this was the layout of what occurred:

I was working out getting ready for the upcoming boating season when I heard this guy make a sound that was almost a yelp. When I turned around I watched this guy fly off the treadmill and another guy sitting on his butt and repeatedly saying "I'm sorry". The guy sitting down got up and went over to the guy who just flew off the treadmill and asked him if was ok. Once it was determined that there were no injuries he started apologizing and stating "I have never had something like this happen to me before".

I stopped my work out and started paying attention to what was going. Apparently the one guy was working out on an exercise ball and the ball shot out from underneath him. Somehow the ball got stuck under the treadmill and basically locked up the treadmill from working. Due to the ball wedging under the treadmill the other guy was shot off and the two of them were trying to sort out how it happened and how they were ever going to get the ball out from its wedged location. I starting snickering and had to bail on my work out before I burst into a full-blown laughter and further embarrassed the two guys.

Barbie's an Angel...Blue but still an Angel

When riding the GO train you really need to make an effort to not get to know the people around you. As a commuter train many people figure you just get on, sit down and then get up when you arrive at your destination which is usually Union Station in downtown Toronto for most people. This couldn't be further from the truth. The same riders sit in the same cars and in the same seats whenever possible. For many riders this is routine (in my case for 6 years it has been the routine). When you have scenarios like this you wind up talking to people and getting to know them. Friendships develop and blossom on the GO train probably due to the train's notorious inefficiency so everyone has a common talking point when things go wrong.

So one afternoon, a Friday right before Hallowe'en a few years ago actually, Barbie and I were joined for lunch with a few of our GO train friends at the Jack Astor's restaurant on Front Street. Barbie walked in with her costume that she wore to work which was that of an angel outfit with a feathery halo and feathery wings. Did I mention that these feathers were a baby blue in colour?

Barbie took her seat at the table and we were kind of snickering at the table a little bit. After taking her seat all the talk was over Barbie's costume.

"How do you like my outfit?" Barbie asked everyone.

"Um, it's cute and kinda funny," one of us replied.

"What do you mean 'funny'?"

"Seriously? You weren't joking with this?"

Barbie was a tad perplexed. "I don't get it", she said.

Our one friend chipped in "Well you are an angel, and you're blue"

"Yeah", said Barbie.

"An angel and blue", was the retort.

"I don't get it. I'm an angel and blue", replied Barbie.

"Yeah! You are a blue angel", our friend said.

"I know. I wanted the pink costume but I couldn't find the halo to match so I bought blue." Barbie answered.

"No, no. I don't think you get it. You are a *Blue Angel*"

"Yeah, I get that. I'm a blue angel. I don't see what all the fuss...", and Barbie stopped mid-sentence when she finally made the connection that her cute little outfit was also the name for a gag teenagers pull when they 'fart' onto an open flame, usually from a lighter. Yes Barbie was a blue angel.

Engineering Barbie and the Reconstructive Surgery

The other day we were sitting around at lunch and talking about accidents and the damage they can cause. This great conversational piece came about from the safety video that we watched about overhead cranes. During this conversation Engineering Barbie curried in about her friends experience.

"I had a friend who had to get reconstructive surgery after a car accident. You'd never knew she had it done except she looks different now"

We all sat around a little dumb-founded after that.

I'll Take "Barbie, Bounce Sheets and Kleenex" For $500, Alex

Today I felt the need to blow my nose since apparently I'm not done with this fall season's allergies. When I wandered over to the Kleenex box and grabbed the next available piece of tissue paper I had a bit of a surprise come out of the box at me. Flying through air was a Bounce sheet that was apparently stuffed into the Kleenex box. I was slightly taken aback at the sight of having an aerial assailant from the tissue box. However, since such sheets don't have much in the way of flight longevity, it begin to flit its way down to the floor. I wandered over and picked up the would-be assassin and looked at it wondering what had happened. The internal Sherlock Holmes in me managed to piece it together fairly quickly as to what did occur.

"Why did you put a Bounce sheet into the Kleenex box?" I asked Barbie.

"Uh, I didn't" Barbie answered.

"Really? Because I'm pretty sure you were the one folding the laundry on Sunday"

"SO! That doesn't mean that I would have put a Bounce sheet there. I mean, why would I?"

"Ok, so who did put it there? Because I'm pretty sure I saw you place them on the table"

"That doesn't mean anything...and besides I probably thought it was a Kleenex that fell out of the box Mr. Smarty Pants."

In unrelated news, the air I've been breathing all has a spring time freshness to it.

Barbies Who Will Never Be Confused With Magellan

The other night we were sitting around watching television when Barbie decided to make dinner. It seems that Barbie had found a neat little Tex-Mex rice dish on-line and she wanted to try making it and see if it was any good. So we made up some taco seasoned ground beef, rice, and vegetables which were then thrown into a casserole dish topped with nacho chips and cheese.

"Dinner's ready", Barbie said. "Maybe we can watch it with that show we've been watching. What's it called...Justified."

"Sure, I'll turn on Netflix", I answered.

"Yep, a Tex-Mex meal while we watch Texas marshals", Barbie said.

I was rather confused by this and let Barbie know that. "You do realize this show takes place in Kentucky right?"

"What do you mean? He has cowboy hats and boots. Plus he has an accent."

"Everyone south of Cincinnati has a southern accent. The Carolinas, Georgia, Tennessee, Louisiana...all have southern accents."

"Well that puts a damper on having a theme dinner doesn't it", Barbie stated as she walked back to the kitchen for the food.

This, however, reminded me of an instance when I use to drive up and down the US east coast wrestling. I was driving down to the Blue Ridge mountain area of North Carolina and I stopped at a rest station in Virginia. This gas stop was advertised as the last one before the state line. So I filled up and went it to pay for my gas when I had the following conversation:

"I'm looking at the map here and it looks like the state line is about an hour and a half or possibly two hours away. Is that about right?" I asked of the attendant.

With what can be described as 'deer in headlights' the lady behind the counter stared at me and with a stereotypical southern drawl responded "Oh, I don't know. I don't get out a lot"

To say I was flabbergasted would be putting it mildly. "Shouldn't information like this be part of your training orientation? Being the last gas station and all?"

I was met with a look that told me I had reached the intellectual capacity of this poor soul and just left my money on the counter and walked away.

Chinese Barbie Needs Remedial Stroller Training

This morning I went with a co-worker to a small little restaurant near my work called Pestos (University and Elm in Toronto). Generally we head over there whenever we are looking for something for breakfast since I can get a toasted western and tea for under $5, which is awesome in Toronto were a Ritz Cracker can go for a bar of gold.

While we were leaving we saw a Chinese lady pushing a baby stroller toward the main entrance of the office building that Pestos is part of. As she approached the entrance we never paid much attention until we heard the cries of dismay behind us. We turned around to see what was going on and what caught our eye was somewhat alarming. The lady was stuck inside the revolving door with her stroller in the quartered section ahead of her and no longer moving. It seems the wheels got stuck while making the rotation and thus locking the mother, or sitter, was stuck.

Frantically the woman was pushing on the door in both directions trying to catch a break of good fortune and have the doors rotate in either direction. As we started walking back another lady had come up to the door and witnessed the debacle. She went over one of the two doors that opened up as a normal door would and walked into the building. From there she removed the stroller and let the lady get herself out of her self-created prison.

I have to be absolutely honest that I started laughing once the whole thing was done. To me, and too many I know, it would seem common sense to use one of the regular doors when pushing a baby stroller...or I'm giving humanity way too much credit for intelligence.

Male Barbies + Loading Docks = Fails and Hilarity

Yesterday when I was at work I bumped into a co-worker after making my lunch trip to Tim Horton's for a cup of tea. Fred, as we will call him, was coming off the elevator that goes from the loading dock to the basement where my machine shop is located. Since most of my team was at a mandatory safety training seminar I was somewhat shocked to see Fred.

"Aren't you doing the safety thing today?"

"No, I signed up for the next session coming up" he replied. "Um, do you know if SPD (our shipping area) has keys to open the loading dock doors?"

"They might. Why?"

"I can't get it to open up. The other door is open but is occupied with a delivery and the truck I'm trying to receive is in the other one."

I was a little confused by all this since I have never seen the loading dock have the garage doors locked during day time hours.

"Really? Let's go see if I can fix you up"

So we got into the elevator and rode up to the loading docks. As we walked over to the dock's doors it was just as he described: one open and one closed. We approached the closed-door and Fred went to open it up.

"See", he said. "It won't open."

I watched as Fred hit the button a few more times and I instantly knew his problem. Fred had been hitting the wrong button. Instead of hitting the **Open** button, which would raise the door up, he was hitting the **Up** button which lifts the tailgate so that you can unload skids from the trucks. I quickly pointed this out to Fred and after sensing his embarrassment I said it would be our secret...until now.

Sauble Barbie and the Discount Ticket War…well skirmish

Today at work Barbie received a call from her co-worker, and previous guest on the blog, Sauble Barbie. It seems Sauble Barbie had purchased some tickets from one of those work perk groups that offer discount deals to employees. Upon ordering she called up Barbie and asked if she wanted to meet up with her while she picked up her order.

Being as they work for one of the larger banks in Toronto our two Barbies do not work in the same building so they met up at the main office where Sauble Barbie thought she could grab her order. Not knowing, however, what floor she needed to go to she approached the concierge desk and asked them. They informed her that she needed to head to the 13th floor, which is never good, and see the folks at Oxford Properties. So off they went together to the 13th floor so that Sauble Barbie could obtain her order.

Upon reaching the 13th floor the two Barbies asked what office it was they needed to go to for ticket pick-ups. Once they got their directions off they went to see the perks agent. As they approached the man at the desk Sauble Barbie handed the gentleman her print out and said "I'm here to get my order".

"Um, this isn't from us", said the agent. "These are from Eservus…you know, our competitor."

A little shell-shocked, and mildly embarrassed, Sauble Barbie asked the agent, "Well, do you know where I can find their office then?"

The perks agent from Oxford admitted that he had no idea where the office for Eservus was but told them that they could use the telephone to call them. He was quite quick to add, being the consummate salesman, that he could get them cheaper than what Sauble Barbie got them for. Sauble Barbie was insistent that there was no way because she bought them on a discount, oblivious to the fact that this was exactly what this gentleman's job detail was as well. After a little tit-for-tat between Sauble Barbie and Oxford's Willie Loman they actually found that Sauble Barbie got the tickets cheaper by 14 cents.

After calling Eservus Sauble Barbie found out that the office she had to go to and receive her tickets was located...

drumroll

In the neighbouring building she works in and therefore she probably never needed to venture outside with Toronto's extensive underground pathways.

The Cold Affects Barbie's Brain

I have to be honest with everyone. If not for the live, commercial free airing of WWE Smackdown then I would have had two posts not one. In saying that here's the great couple of days that have surrounded Barbie and her adventurous spirit in Toronto.

Tuesday

Barbie got to work and went through her usual routine of setting up her desk, since her work is too cheap to have permanent desks for everyone, and getting sorted out for the work day. All things seemed to go according to plan that is until lunch time. At lunch time it all went awry. When it was time for lunch Barbie went to the office kitchen and opened the fridge. Pondering for a while, because something seemed wrong, she stared at the fridge. Finally it clicked in - her lunch was missing. Instantly Barbie figured someone stole her food. Quickly scanning the other office workers, Barbie channelled her inner Encyclopaedia Brown and tried to figure out who was the thief. As Barbie was doing the 'over the cubicle head scan' trying to sort out who was the culprit something inside her head was saying "You're getting colder". Unfortunately for poor Barbie this voice wasn't playing that stand-by game of "Getting Warmer, Getting Colder" with her. This was a clue. It turns out that Barbie, in a moment of absent-mindedness, she placed her lunch inside the freezer of the fridge instead of the regular fridge part.

Wednesday

Today was a rather good day...or it was until about 3.45pm. I grabbed Barbie from her place of work on the way to the GO Train and we took off down York Street toward Union Station. We were passing the Sigma Building at 55 York Street when all of a sudden Barbie dropped like Joe Frazier. It seems that due to some brilliant construction work, or really shoddy engineering, there is quite the difference in height between the sidewalk and sidewalk markers. In fact about 1/2" difference actually, which is nearly 13mm for the metric crowd. To anyone who doesn't know the math apparently, as scientific studies show, all that is needed is 2mm (which is 0.08 inches) difference in height to upset someone's balance. So down she went, mild injury to the ankle and that is all thankfully, and I was standing over Barbie. After helping her up, and making sure she was ok, we went off to the GO Train.

We made the train in time to get a seat, which is crucial on our line, and awaited the usual crowd that we sit with. It seems we are the only suckers working this week since they didn't arrive. Barbie, having been out with some former co-workers, had a few extra bags of stuff with today. So we bundled ourselves into the seats and did the best we could to get our bags, as well as the extra bags, under seats to eliminate the encroachment into the sitting space of the other riders. This posed a problem. The problem isn't that we couldn't fit the bags under and leave our co-commuters the appropriate space but rather that we were able to accomplish such a feat. As we pulled into our stop, which caught Barbie off guard and this might have been part of the issue, Barbie scrambled to shut down her e-reader and get her bags together. We scrambled off the train and as we were walking down the platform Barbie turned to me and said "Oh good. You have my backpack"

I looked rather confused at her and replied "No I don't. I have my own backpack and one of the extra bags but not your backpack".

As the train was pulling away from us Barbie realized that her backpack, complete with laptop, notebooks and such, was sitting under our chairs on the train that was slowly pulling away to the west.

Barbie Has a Cat Burglar

So the other day Barbie was separating her Christmas gifts into the piles of whom they would be going to. Basically she had piles for the various family members as well as for the pets. Barbie had taken one of those piles down to the living room, which she had staged as the wrapping station. Suddenly she hears this thud upstairs which was followed by a set of little thuds. As she "arose to hear such a clatter", after all we need some Christmas theme here, Barbie noticed that her cat Dexter had dug out the toy hedgehog that was to be his Christmas gift. The hedgehog was still attached to its cardboard packaging and he was tossing it down the stairs and chasing it. So, as the saying goes, curiosity killed the cat or in this case killed his surprise Christmas gift. So the lesson learnt is not only do people need to hide their gifts from their children but also from their dogs and cats.

Barbie Stars in "Attack of the Killer Cheeseburgers"

On Friday night Barbie's brother called up to let her know he was popping over but was hitting McDonald's first and asked her if she wanted anything to eat. Barbie told him no she was fine since she had a cheeseburger for lunch. So Todd, who previously appeared in the Genealogy post, came by with a cheeseburger anyway.

"I told you I didn't want a cheeseburger. I already had one at lunch", Barbie told Todd when he walked in.

"Yeah and previously you always gave me crap when I would come by and not have one for you. So here, take it."

Barbie didn't want the burger at the time so she placed it in the fridge for future consumption.

The next day she decided she would warm it up for lunch. Taking the burger from the fridge she placed it in the microwave and set the timer on it for 90 seconds. The reasoning for this was Barbie wanted to make sure it was thoroughly cooked through, even though the burger was already cooked just the night before. Her concern is that she would get food poisoning if it wasn't cooked right through. Let's remember, as per Barbie Has a Meltdown, she is a bit of a hypochondriac.

So 90 seconds later and a burger heated to the point of setting of a Geiger counter sees Barbie sit down for lunch. By the third bite, which would get you to the middle of the burger, Barbie found herself in a bit of a hot pickle. Well, more accurately the pickle that was on the burger came lose, slapped Barbie in the mouth and the overheated cheese gave Barbie a great burn across her bottom lip. With some yelping from the scalding received Barbie took off to get some salve on her lips to mitigate the damage. The lesson learnt is eat your burger when it's fresh boys and girls.

Barbie and the Brain Eating Amoeba

Hello everyone. It has been a very long time since I've put any story up and it most certainly isn't because we haven't had Barbie moments but more because in the pursuit of obtaining certification as a Project Manager I was taking two different night school courses, which are over (thank God).

So a few weeks back, probably around 8 weeks ago to be honest, I got an email from Barbie at my work because she was somewhat flustered. It seems that Barbie had ingested a brain eating amoeba...or so she thought.

Barbie, at the time, was suffering somewhat of a nasal condition and was using Hydrasense to flush out her sinuses to reduce infection. Enter the moment when Rod Serling does his Twilight Zone voice over and the familiar musically twang hits...yes we've hit "*The Barbie Zone*".

It seems that Barbie had run out of Hydrasense, not surprising if you remember the Bukkake story, and decided on doing a homemade Neti Pot. So Barbie boiled some water, let it cool off and made a nasal rinse using some sea salt. After creating this concoction she performed her Charlie Sheen impersonation and performed a nasal rinse from it. So far so good. It was after this that all plans went to pot.

Barbie, with her ever vigilante internet medical searches, found this article which describe a brain eating amoeba found in tap water. Of course having read this article Barbie was convinced she had contracted it. However, after reading this article (which she read as well) remember the following:

- the deaths were in Louisiana
- less than 10 reported cases occur per year (in the US)
- the highest number of reported incidents were 8 in 1980
- the amoeba is a warm water friendly amoeba with very rare cases reported north of the Mason-Dixie Line

To make a long story short I received a rather panicked email from Barbie concerned because she had found out this information but, of course, after the nasal rinsing had taken place. No matter what was said I couldn't settle Barbie down from the fact that she may have 'snorted' a brain eating amoeba. In fact it might have been easier to give a logical explanation as to how all the grass is freshly cut in "*The Walking Dead*" than have Barbie believe that she wasn't in harm's way from this homemade nasal rinse. So the countdown began since the amoeba would kill a person in 7 days. Barbie went as far as emailing the town to find out the chlorination levels of water treatment because certain levels would kill the amoeba. She also asked her OBGYN about it and that didn't go so well (only because the good doctor laughed at her).

So the longest week of my life then began. With each passing day I would hear about the countdown - "I might die in 6 days". Of course I never believed it but someone did (nudge, nudge, wink, wink). So day after day went by and numbers slowly dropped with an anticipation I can only expect was matched by the original moon landing.

To say the least, nothing happened to Barbie. We are now working on about day 60+ after the nasal rinse but I will testify how bent out of shape Barbie was.

Barbie's Medical Problems while being Preggers

This pregnancy has most certainly been a trying one. Trying for poor Barbie because it's given her more reasons to look up medical maladies and trying for me because I get to bear the brunt of these, as Barbie so eloquently puts it, "her irrational thoughts of the week ".

Barbie had been suffering some tightness and cramping due to a combination of Braxton-Hicks contractions and the growing of all things uteral. So when explaining this problem to her OB, the doctor told her to use a heating pad to ease up the tightening of muscles and create some comfort. So out came the heating pad. For weeks Barbie would place the heating pad on her stomach when problems were starting. The funniest of all this was that Dexter, the cat, would fight her for the heating pad. Every time she'd get up you would see the cat sneak over and stretch himself across the heating pad to enjoy a nice warm pseudo-bed.

About 9 or 10 weeks of this went by before Barbie stumbled across an article on the great and glorious internet. It turns out that the heating pad should have never been on her stomach at all but on her back. As she was reading this article the only thing missing was the voice over from Cape Canaveral. "T-minus 10 seconds to Barbie meltdown"

Sure enough the meltdown began within seconds of her finishing this lovely piece of web-based news.

"I think I've melted the baby", she blurted.

"Oh yeah," I responded. "And why's that?"

"I was supposed to have the heating pad on my back not my stomach."

Like a fish I took the bait. "Go on..." I said.

"Nobody told me it had to be my back. My stomach was the part tightening up, not my back. Nobody said anything so I've been heating my stomach. And now I think I've boiled the baby."

At this point in the conversation I went to grab a cold beer out of the fridge. (Thank you Budweiser, you've been a pal these last 8 months)

"You've not boiled the baby", I told her. "The baby is fine."

"No, I think I might have boiled the baby. Or maybe cooked its little organs. What if I made it retarded?"

"Call the doctor, tell her what you think you've done and I bet I'm right."

So the next morning Barbie gets in touch with the doctor and spills her guts out. She mentions the cooking of babies, the not knowing about placing the heating pad on her back not her stomach and how distraught she was. The doctor said not to worry the baby is fine. It is very well protected in there and she would have done more harm to herself before doing any harm to the baby. At least the doctor didn't snicker at her like she did with the brain-eating amoeba.

I Should Have Gotten a Puppy

I have to deeply apologize for not updating this blog since April 16th however we have had a whirlwind month and a bit. On April 22nd Barbie and I had a baby boy named Alexander who weighed 6lb 13oz. Since then we've had a few Barbie-esque moments, and as anyone who has had children before can attest, time has not really been much of a freedom when you have someone looking to eat every 2 to 3 hours and needing diaper changes every 2 hours as well.

So we'll start at the beginning - the day of delivery. Barbie checked for inducement at 8.00am on the 22nd at the local hospital. By 8.30am everything was set in motion. By 1pm I had arrived at the hospital from work to take part in the 'miracle of birth'. Things were moving along rather slowly and discussions had started about using Pitocin, epidurals and manually breaking Barbie's water. So we waited, and waited, and waited for nature to take its proper course.

By 4pm the OB/GYN came into the room and decided that he didn't want to wait any longer. He took a seat like he was playing Texas Hold'em and before I knew it a sound akin to the River Nile was in the room. So the water was broke and things finally were set in motion...so I thought.

By 7pm not a single thing happened. So step number two occurred. One of the nurses came in and hooked up am Pitocin IV drip to speed things up. Actually it turns out to have been oxytocin, which should not be confused with OxyContin as any lady who has been in labour can attest to.

By 8pm the anesthesiologist came in to insert the epidural drip. Realistically the whole procedure should have taken 15 to 20 minutes. Instead we had 3 attempts, 3 different holes and a pregnant Barbie who was very sore, very agitated and not a happy camper with the fact that 45 minutes later this guy still couldn't get the epidural to take. Eventually Barbie, who had been sitting up and leaning at a 30 degree angle against me, told him "I've had enough, you need to stop." Defeated the anesthesiologist did the walk of shame out of the room. Barbie muttered painfully at this moment "I should have gotten a puppy instead".

The sitting up had actually done more for Barbie than any of the previous attempts as she opened up from 4cm, as of 8pm, to a whopping 9.5cm by 8.45pm. At about 9.15 one of the assistant nurses came in and asked Barbie to give a little push to see where the baby's head was in terms of coming out. So Barbie pushed as requested and the nurse went "Whoa, you need to stop. That was a great push and this kid's ready to come out." She grabbed the first nurse walking past and told her get the O.B. down here now.

By 9.21 the doctor arrived and things went like wildfire. To start with the bed transformed from being a bed to being a bed with stirrups. It was the wildest thing. The bottom third, where the legs would be obviously, slid out and collapsed. Then these two legs popped up with stirrups on them. The doctor then slide his chair in and took a position like Johnny Bench playing catcher for the Cincinnati Reds. Barbie started pushing and pushing. After about 20 minutes of pushing the head started to crown out.

At the moment the head was coming out the doctor, for reasons only known to him, decided he was working of Ipsos Reid and took a poll. Looking around the room, starting with me, he asked everyone what they thought the baby was a boy or a girl. I said a boy, Barbie's mom said a girl, and Barbie's cousin said a girl would be nice but a boy. Finally Barbie, when asked, what she would like, answered simply

"I just want it out."

Five minutes later the new born baby boy was out and Barbie wasn't so focused on having a new puppy instead.

What's My Name?

A few days after Barbie had given birth she was out at the local Wal-Mart with her mom. While shopping an older lady approached her to fawn over the baby. While cooing over the child the lady posed the question -

"How cute. What did you name him?"

Normally this would be a simple question that the majority of people could answer really quickly. Unfortunately for Barbie, she had literally come out of the hospital the day previously and was working on about 8 hours sleep over the last 3 days. So naturally her response was a little slow.

"Um...his name is...um...mom?"

"His name is Alex", came in mom with the hot tag and rescue.

Barbie Is Still Musically Challenged

I have to be honest considering I haven't heard of most bands after 1992, it is a little rich for me to call Barbie musically challenged but what the heck...she is!!! As the regular readers might remember when Barbie confused Abba with Blondie and Outkast with K'naan we had another classic music confusion last week.

Young Alexander tends to sneer his lip very akin to Billy Idol at times. So during one of these moments I mentioned how he looks very much like Billy Idol and Barbie laughed and agreed. So while I slaughtered the words to Rebel Yell with my angelic singing, or catlike screeching, Barbie had little Alexander's arm pumping like Billy Idol's does in his videos.

When I finished singing the course of "More, More, More", and in all honestly stopped singing all together due to not knowing the words after that, Barbie chimed in with her own song.

"School's out for summer..."

I cocked my head sideways rather confused and queried "Alice Cooper?!?!?!?"

"Um, I thought that was Billy Idol"

"No, that's Alice Cooper. Maybe you meant 'It's a nice day for a white wedding' or 'Here she comes now singing mony, mony'?

"Uh, yeah that is what I meant"

However, I could tell by the look in her eye she was really singing "Hey Ya" by Outkast

Barbie and the Urban Poling

Today I was reading the latest community activity guide that came to the house. I was reading out the extreme lack of programs available for anyone over 18.

"Listen to the vast amount of activities we can sign up for", I said sarcastically.   " We have spin classes, yoga, pilates, power half-hour and urban poling."

"OMG, you know what that is right?" asked Barbie. "That's that pole dancing aerobic thingie"

"Um, no. It's some new thing where you walk around with large poles like you are cross country skiing almost." I then showed her a picture of it from the guide.

"You're going to blog this aren't you?" Barbie asked hoping I'd refuse the bait. However, I just smiled and nodded.
"Oh yeah, this is getting published"

Dexter the Cat – Secretly gay or an avid R. Kelly fan?

On Monday night, after scrambling around collecting the garbage, recycling and compost waste, we were getting ready for bed and I noticed that Dexter the cat didn't come running for a night treat when I let the dog outside for a final bathroom break. Not thinking a lot of it I went back upstairs and went to bed. While lying in bed I asked Barbie if she had seen the cat lately.

"No actually. He didn't come running when I put out his dinner either but I'm sure he has eaten it."

We laid there for a little while and I decided that no this was too weird and I was going to find the cat. I looked behind our bed - nothing. So I went to my teenage son's room and checked his closet and under his bed - nothing. I went into the baby's room and checked under the crib and in the closet - nothing. So I went downstairs to the kitchen and grabbed the bag of Temptations Cat Treats and started walking around the main floor shaking it while looking behind couches and entertainment centres all to no avail. My last check was the basement. Down I went, shaking the treat bag the whole time, and checked behind the washer, dryer, in among the boxes, behind mattresses that are stored there and could not find a single clue.

I went back up to the kitchen to put the treat bag back and noticed that the cat's food had not been touched. Resigning myself to the fact that Dexter, who is agoraphobic, may have mustered up the spine to actually go outside for a sniff while the dog was doing her thing and was locked out there because nobody noticed him sneak outside because it is so against his normal behaviour. I made my way back to the bedroom to get changed so I could walk around and look outside and broke the news to Barbie that the cat's food was untouched and I'm going to look outside. As I was making my way back to the stair case I realized the one place I didn't look was in the linen closet.

I had often seen Dexter, and shooed him out there, climbing in the closet to snuggle amid the towels and blankets. I opened the door up and sitting two shelves up from the floor, laying on top of some towels was Dexter and he started letting out sympathetic "meows". I took him out of there and downstairs to eat. He was pretty noisy that night as if he was giving both of us crap for his ordeal. So the questions lies "Did the cat come out of the closet? Or was he trapped in the closet?"

I Can Sing a Rainbow...well Barbie couldn't

The other day Barbie and I were sitting watching TV, well let's be honest with a 7 month old in the house we really only watch two things - Baby Einstein DVDs and the toddler channel Treehouse. So in watching one of these DVDs there was a rainbow showing up on-screen and I had a flashback to my days of music class in grade school.

Without missing a beat my memory banks pulled out the words for the song "I Can Sing a Rainbow". So, in my very best attempt to not totally butcher the song, I began singing:

"Red and yellow and pink and green, purple and orange and blue, I can sing a rainbow..."

At this moment I was cut off by Barbie. Not because I was committing auditory murder to a song that is 58 years old but because I "apparently" had the wrong lyrics.

"You mixed the colours up. It goes red, yellow, purple and blue, pink, orange and green."

I paused for a half-second and then looked at Barbie and said "Um, no. It ends it blue. I had it right"

"It can't end in blue. Blue doesn't make sense, it has to end with green", was the retort from Barbie.

This went on for about 2 or 3 minutes with the verdict being we had to ask an intellectual authority figure. Barbie emailed her mom while I went to the internet. The results were that Barbie's mom wasn't sure what the order of colours were but according to the internet I was right as proven by a video on YouTube.

Crans? What the heck are 'Crans'?

The other day we were sitting around half-ass watching television. In other words the television was on but we were both doing other things. I was in the middle of conversations with folks from my previous existence and an attempted pro-wrestler and Barbie was...well, Barbie was on her new addiction Pinterest.

"Hey", exclaimed Barbie. "I found this cool way to make your own t-shirt designs"

"Uh-uh", I replied because to be honest I was only quasi-listening.

"Yeah, you get really fine grit sandpaper and draw on your design using crans and then iron it on your shirt."

This caught my attention. "You mean 'crayons'?" I asked.

"Pfft, nobody says 'crayons'. It's crans."

"What? 'Crans'? Really? Like some sort of Ocean Spray drink? Cran-Pomegranate? Nobody, outside of you says 'crans'. Its crayons. Cray...Ons. Two syllables. Like 'A Tribe Called Quest' you have to say the whole thing!"

This kept on for a few minutes about who was right and ended with Barbie saying she was going to email her mom for conformation on how it's pronounced. Her mom has avoided getting mixed up in this one...probably because she's still laughing at 'crans'.

Let Me Introduce You to Presidents Edmund Fitzgerald and Thomas Edison

So as I type this Barbie and I are watching "Scandal" on Netflix. The episode we are watching they showed a flashback where the president was being sworn in. In the show the president is named Fitzgerald Thomas Grant. Once they announced his full-name I made the comment "Wow, all names from former presidents."

Barbie then chimed in and said "Yep. Ulysses S. Grant. Edmund Fitzgerald..."

"What? Edmund Fitzgerald was a boat", I told her.

"Uh? It was a person too"

"Um, a boat in a song that was sung by Gordon Lightfoot. The president would be John Fitzgerald Kennedy hence the "F" in John F. Kennedy"

"Oh, and is it...Thomas..."

"Jefferson", I told her.

"Oh, so not Edison"

Hi Ho Tonto!!!

So today we were playing with our son in the living room turned toy room with all his recently acquired haul from his first birthday party last weekend. One of his toys that he's taken to is a Fisher-Price Little People Farm with lots of audio stimuli. The farm itself comes with a little farmer, a horse, a cow, a bale of hay and a sheep. Alex likes to open the gates up, because they make animal sounds, and drop things down the silo because there is a sensor at the bottom which triggers various sounds and songs.

While playing our son took the horse and was waving it around. I had stepped into the kitchen at the time and I heard Barbie say

"Hi Ho Tonto away!"

Needless to say I stopped dead in my tracks and muttered, well maybe louder than mutter, out "Wow. Tonto huh?"

"Yeah, he's got the horse", stated Barbie.

"Um, Tonto is not the horse"

"Wait, what? So what was the horse's name?" asked Barbie.

"Well Tonto was the Indian", I replied. And yes I know it isn't PC but we all know it as Lone Ranger and his Indian pal Tonto not his native pal.

"Ooh." Then out of the blue Barbie had a neuron connection occur and she snapped out, "Silver! The horse was Silver"

"Yep. And what was Tonto's horse called?"

"Tonto had a horse?"

"Of course he had a horse. Did you think he ran behind the Lone Ranger in a pair of Nike's? The horse was called Scout"

Barbie also realized what was happening at that moment, "You better blog this one."

And ta-da, your wish is my command!!!

The Smiths

A few weeks ago we were watching TV and an odd conversation about names came about and how they were related to the trade or service a person worked at.

As we went about it the name Smith came up:

"Yeah Smith was for those who were blacksmiths", I said.

"And candlesmiths", Barbie added.

"Candlesmiths?" I asked.

"Yeah. You know the butcher, the baker and the candlesmith maker."

At that moment the light bulb in Barbie's head went off as she realized it just didn't sound right.

"Candlesmith? You mean candlestick maker don't you?" I asked her.

"Um, aren't they also a smith?" she asked hoping for a lifeline here.

"Nope. Although next time I play Clue I will call for Professor Plum in the Billiard Room with a candlesmith."

No wonder I get the couch a lot.

The Genealogy Lessons Continue

On the weekend we were up at a trailer outside of Huntsville, Ontario visiting friends. During this trip we almost had a transport to the Barbie zone. We were eating and watching some TV, since it was pouring rain out and we were somewhat locked in, when Barbie piped up.

"You know I was just thinking I didn't know what Mike's last name is."

Mike has the trailer across the way from the one we were staying at and often sits with us during the nightly campfires, weather permitting.

"You're kidding me" said Barbie's friend to her. "You really didn't know what his last name was?"

"Well, the more I thought about it I realized it had to be the same as Paul's name"

Paul and Mike are brothers. It was a close call and would have definitely been a better conversation piece if she hadn't had her revelation.

Barbie Doesn't Do Terrorist Attractions

Tonight, after dinner, Barbie and I went for a walk through the neighbourhood. As we were walking Barbie started talking about some recent business trips she might going off on. One of which is London, England and she mentioned how when she goes she wants to 'do it right' and have a pint, eat some crumpets and hit Piccadilly Circus. During this I said to her that if she wanted to do London right she had to use London's subway system The Tube.

"Oh no", Barbie said. "I can't go on that."

"Relax. It much easier to use and ride than the TTC (Toronto's subway)", I replied.

"No, it's not that. It's a terrorist attraction!"

"A terrorist attraction?" I asked.

"Yeah a place that attracts terrorists."

"It's not Al Qaeda-land for Pete's sake*. Mickey Mouse in an exploding vest and all that nonsense."

"It's a place that attracts terrorists so it's a terrorist attraction"

"I believe the actual term is a terrorist target not attraction"

'Whatever. They are attracted to it so I'm not wrong"

I had to concede on that point but not without a good laugh

*phrase not actually used but we're keeping it family oriented ;)

Barbie's Musical Follies Continue

The other night we were watching an old episode of the Comedy Central show Tosh.0 featuring Daniel Tosh. If you haven't watched this show I highly recommend it. Tosh's less than politically correct comedy mixed with the internet's petri dish of Darwin Award contenders and the videos they post makes for some great laughable moments.

During this episode somebody, and I think it was Tosh, said the line "We didn't start the fire". Of course this set our little blonde jukebox into song.

"You didn't start the fire"

Perplexed I made a comment and then asked the pertinent question.

"The line is 'we didn't start the fire' and do you even know who sung that song?" To be honest I was playing the age factor here in assuming she wouldn't know who sung it. To be honest I was amazed she even knew the song since it came out in 1989 when Barbie would have been 8 years old.

"Yes. It was Billy..." And the pause occurred whilst Barbie racked her brain to find the correct artist that would correlate with the correct song.

"Billy who? There's only few of them. Idol, Squires, Joel."

"Idol. Yeah Billy Idol." She has stated it with a bit of pride.

"The blond spiky haired guy from *The Wedding Singer* who sings Mony, Mony? No try Billy Joel"

"Are you sure?" she asked.

"Positive. He wrote the song about all the major events that happened in his life to commemorate his 40th birthday. He also sang Uptown Girl and Piano Man."

Barbie gave me a look at that moment which pretty much said she didn't know those songs.

Other musical fails from Barbie are:

Confusing Alice Cooper with *drumroll*...Billy Idol

Barbie messing up the colours for the song I Can Sing a Rainbow

Barbie confusing Abba with Blondie

Barbie thinking Credence Clearwater Revival and California Raisins were the same band...although it was the same song

And lastly confusing K'naan with Outkast

Barbie's Introduction to the World of Pro Wrestling

For those unaware I spent a good amount of time wrestling on what is called the 'Indy' circuit, meaning independent...basically independent of WWE. I had stepped away back in 2004 for various personal reasons but as of late have become reacquainted with the scene. One of my favourite promoters was retiring due to health issues and I agreed to slap on the boots, and according to Barbie way too much spandex, for one final hurrah.

A few weeks later we had a team meeting at my place of work and on the final slide, entitled questions, was a picture of me from that final match laying a beating on my opponent. So when I came home I told Barbie all about it. I mentioned that they had the photo up from the match where I was performing a move, made famous by The Iron Sheik, called The Camel Clutch. This is where the Barbie-ism began.

"Is that the move where you grab him between the legs?" Barbie asked.

"Uh? Ok, first off I never grabbed that guy between the legs in that match and secondly it was the move where I sat over him and arched his back by pulling up on his chin with his arms trapped between my legs and my arms. It's a Camel Clutch not a Camel Toe Clutch."

Now a few months after this there was a fundraising dinner for the Pro Wrestling Hall of Fame in Amsterdam, New York. This is an actual physical building with great artifacts and exhibits and is controlled by a board. Don't confuse this with the WWE Hall of Fame that you hear about during Wrestlemania. This dinner, and one year it was a breakfast, has been going on for about 7 years and I've been asked to attend from guys past and present just to hang out. Lord knows I didn't make enough impact to be inducted lol.

So I agreed to go this year and bought two tickets. I had never been but based on the few photos I had seen it looked to be a semi-formal affair so I pulled out my suit and Barbie found a dress. Turns out we could have stepped it down a notch...or three. Some folks were dressed up, others in a more casual attire.

As we were talking to a few guys I've had the pleasure of working with and for I could see Barbie staring around the room in disbelief. So I asked her what her impression was.

"That guy has a mask on. And isn't that guy the one you helped with the ring? And why does this dude have ruby-red cowboy boots?"

"Yes that would be Mac and the guy with the masked is Dick Beyer, better known as The Sensational Destroyer. The guy in the boots is Bobby Bass, or No Class Bobby Bass when he wrestled."

"But why does he have a mask on?"

"He wrestled in a mask so its 'gimmick'."

"But why does he still have it on?"

"Simple, fans are here too and they've never seen his face so the only way to recognize him is through the mask."

"And this guy? That's The Rock's uncle right?"

"Yes it is. And his name is Ricky Johnson. Beside him is his brother, Rocky Johnson."

This seemed to sate her appetite of curiosity. Well until dinner time started. The caterers at the event started bringing out items like ketchup, sour cream and cheese curds. Barbie's interest in the meal suddenly peaked, because I thought it would be standard fare like a roast dinner.

"Please tell me I didn't get dressed up for poutine?"

"Honestly, we might have." I was laughing as I said it.

So dinner came out and there were chicken skewers, roast beef, potatoes and two items Barbie found hilarious – perogies and macaroni with cheese. As dinner began you could see her scouring the room taking in this little soiree because she knew it was like nothing she'd ever been to or seen. To her credit she stayed pretty calm despite having two super-fans beside her just rambling on about wrestling, the shows they've seen and stars they've met. I'd admired her restraint because I'm not sure I'd have been as accommodating if it was a big figure skating affair we went to and I got stuck beside two folks that would ramble on about meeting Elizabeth Manley or Toller Cranston.

"Um, that guy still has his mask on."

"Yep. I'm not surprised"

"But he's eating. Why can't he take it off to eat?"

"Again there are fans here and he doesn't want to show his face. Hell, back in the day these guys came to the arena in a mask, wrestled and then showered in their mask. They had different masks for each task."

"Shut up! They did not!"

So at this moment I leaned over to my trainer, Smith Hart of the famous Hart family, and said to him "Hey, she doesn't believe me that these guys showered with their masks on"

Smith proceeded to tell her about guys who came and went from Calgary wrestling for his father Stu that Smith had never seen their faces despite wrestling them and sharing locker rooms with them. You could tell she didn't approve but accepted the answer despite it's weirdness. We proceeded to finish our dinner and then listen to speeches from Rocky Johnson and Sweet Daddy Siki, whom they were honouring, as well as the fine emcee skills of author Greg Oliver.

Afterwards we mingled around and talked to legends I haven't seen in over a decade. Guys like Siki, Destroyer, Chuck Simms, Terry Dart and Wolfman Willie Farkas. I introduced Barbie to Rocky Johnson and Willie Farkas. Willie used to take my 15-year-old son, who would have been 3 or 4 at the time, and teach him how to wrestle before the shows would start. I also got to meet Tim Gerrard and a personal favourite of mine 'Silent' Brian Mackney. Brian was nicknamed silent because he was legitimately deaf. After trying this career I realized just how much harder he had to work to be good because of his condition. However the best conversation I had that night was with High-flying Bobby Marshall. Marshall, a Hamilton boy, wrestled in the 60's and was a friend of another guy I used to train with 'The Executioner' Ernie Moore and we spoke for about 15 minutes about nothing but the great Lou Thesz.

When we left to go home, from a night I completely enjoyed but Barbie not so much due to the bizarre nature of events from a world she can't really believe exists as it does. The first thing I heard was

"You owe me big time. Fancy restaurants, chick flicks, spa days...you can't say no after this. And if anyone ever asks me if I can smell what The Rock is cooking I can say perogies."

Pretty sure she was laughing maniacally once she said this too.

Barbie Fails at Cultural Greetings

At Barbie's place of work she's been tasked with a large project involving her company's global offices as well as the Canadian ones. As a side result she's had many emails and phone calls with associates in the United States and the United Kingdom. Including trips booked to both locations for work.

During one of these phone calls to an associate in London, England Barbie opened the conversation with "Top O'morning". The associate gave a polite chuckle and thanked her. When Barbie got home she told me about the conversation and I started snickering.

"You do realize that the phrase you used is an Irish greeting not an English one right?"

"Wait…I did what? Oh, man I'm going to need a cheat sheet of what to say and what things are called aren't I?"

"Yeah it probably wouldn't hurt. But at least you know now not to say 'Top O'morning' to anyone."

Thankfully she's not going anywhere that could cause a diplomatic incident with her Barbie-isms.

Barbie is definitely not Magellan

We were sitting down discussing the Ebola outbreak and Barbie was concerned due to her friend doing work in Ethiopia. Due to the outbreak hitting 4 or 5 countries she was concerned that her friend may come in contact with someone carrying the disease.

"What if she comes back with Ebola?"

"She's not coming back with Ebola. She isn't even on the same coast."

"Yeah but she's in Africa so she's got to be close, right?"

"Look, the western coast has the outbreak and it's contained to the five countries in that one region. Ethiopia is on the eastern front near the Suez Canal". This was met with a bit of a blank stare. "You know, close to the Middle East? And Africa is huge. You do know how many countries are in Africa right?"

"Yeah, of course. It's got like 20 countries doesn't it?"

"Try closer to 54. South America has the least with 12 or 13 if you don't count Australia since it's a country and continent. You can name the ones in South America right?"

"Uh, yeah. There's Mexico and Brazil and..."

"Mexico isn't South America. It's North America."

"But its south and south of America"

I walked away giggling and definitely feeling burning eyes in my back.

Barbie Gets Ebola and a Geography Lesson

The other night Barbie comes in from work just fuming and rather exasperated. Of course I ask why, although really if I had waited 5 more seconds she would have went off about it anyways.

"I hate people", is how the conversation started.

"Ok, I'll bite. Why do you hate people?"

"I went to use the bathroom on the train and I was in a rush so I didn't check first", Barbie exclaimed.

I should have let her finish but I didn't and chipped in, "Let me guess, there was no paper in the dispensers?"

"No, this goof peed on the seat and I sat in it." This was said with a mixture of frustration and angst. I started snickering, albeit not quite out loud yet. "I think I might have Ebola now."

Cue the full blown laughter. "And why do we have Ebola?"

"Because I sat in pee. And bodily fluid is one way it can be transported." In her defence she is somewhat right but she also suffers medical anxiety where she thinks she's going to catch everything.

"That doesn't mean you will get it. How the heck do you even know he had it?"

"I saw his work badge. He works at the hospital, you know the one that is always sending people overseas on the 'do-gooder' work. Remember how many nurses and doctors from the train went to Haiti? For all I know he was one of the ones in Africa!"

"Do you have this same panic when you go see your own doctor?"

Barbie looked perplexed and answered, "No. Why would I? She's from Egypt."

Having played this game a long time I knew we had a Barbie moment in the making. "Um, you do realize that Egypt is in Africa right?"

"What?!? I thought it was its own country?"

"It is its own country", now I was getting confused.

"No...like Australia is."

"Oh, you mean a continent. No, it's a country. In Africa."

"But she doesn't look African!"

"It's in North Africa. You know near the Middle East...right across the Suez Canal" By her look I could tell she wasn't catching what I was saying. "Ok let me put it this way Egypt is closer to Greece than it is Mali or Nigeria. This is also why Egyptians tend to look more Arabic or even southern Greek or Italian. Remember the whole story of Marc Anthony and Cleopatra?"

You could tell by her look she didn't. And as she walked away you could see the gears in her head churning out this information for the probability of virus travel.

Made in the USA
Charleston, SC
27 December 2014